Brenda George

Rejoicing through the Tears

Embracing God's Hand in Cancer

Brenda George

Copyright © 2011 Brenda George

All rights reserved. No part of this book may be used or reproduced by any means, graphic, electronic, or mechanical, including photocopying, recording, taping or by any information storage retrieval system without the written permission of the publisher except in the case of brief quotations embodied in critical articles and reviews.

WestBow Press books may be ordered through booksellers or by contacting:

WestBow Press
A Division of Thomas Nelson
1663 Liberty Drive
Bloomington, IN 47403
www.westbowpress.com
1-(866) 928-1240

Because of the dynamic nature of the Internet, any web addresses or links contained in this book may have changed since publication and may no longer be valid. The views expressed in this work are solely those of the author and do not necessarily reflect the views of the publisher, and the publisher hereby disclaims any responsibility for them.

Certain stock imagery © Thinkstock.
Any people depicted in stock imagery provided by Thinkstock are models, and such images are being used for illustrative purposes only.

Scripture taken from the Amplified Bible, Copyright © 1954, 1958, 1962, 1964, 1965, 1987 by The Lockman Foundation. Used by permission.

The information about thyroid cancer has been used with permission by ThyCa, The Thyroid Cancer Survivors' Association, Inc.

Cover design by Sarah George Parks
Book Illustrations by Savannah Cassidy George

ISBN: 978-1-4497-2402-3 (sc)
ISBN: 978-1-4497-2401-6 (hc)
ISBN: 978-1-4497-2400-9 (e)

Library of Congress Control Number: 2011914357

Printed in the United States of America

WestBow Press rev. date: 10/3/2011

Contents

- Foreword vii
- About the Author xi
- Acknowledgments xiii
- Introduction xvii
- Disclaimer xxi

PART ONE: MY LIFE BEFORE THE DIAGNOSIS

1. My Life before Cancer 1
2. The Wedding 19
3. The First Doctor Visit 24
4. The Vacation 26
5. The Diagnosis 34

PART TWO: MY EXPERIENCE WITH THYROID CANCER

6. Life Goes On . . . Or Does It? 39
7. The Surgery 43
8. The Radiation Treatment 47
9. Totally Isolated 50
10. I'll Be Home for Christmas 54
11. The Following Year 57

PART THREE: THERE IS LIFE AFTER A CANCER DIAGNOSIS

12. The Nearness of God 65
13. The Midnight Hour 70
14. Things I've Learned the Hard Way 80
15. You Can Get Fit and Healthy Again 124
16. Keep Looking for Your Rainbow 133
17. An Update 135

PART FOUR: HELPFUL RESOURCES

18. Special Words to Families and Caregivers
    of Thyroid Cancer Patients.. 147
19. Facts and Resources about Thyroid Cancer 151
20. Uplifting Scriptures 180

Foreword

It was a cold, rainy night. I was buckled in the backseat of my mom's car. The windshield wipers were turned on high, and we were headed home. It might have been an ordinary night, but for some reason, it left a lasting impression upon me. My mom began to sing to my sister, brother and I, a very special song, her favorite, sounding like this: "I come to the garden alone while the dew is still on the roses."

In that bittersweet moment, I somehow realized, even at that young age of ten years old, how fragile life is, and I saw my mom as a treasured gift from God. Only he knew for how long I would have her. So I just relaxed and enjoyed the moment. "And the joy we share as we tarry there, none other has ever known."

For my entire life, my mom has been my biggest inspiration and, next to God, my strength. There have been many times that I have needed her to lean on. There were also many times that she could have turned her back on me, but she chose to love me instead. She always saw my good qualities, yet she didn't ignore my faults. But instead of putting me down, she pulled me up. She taught me important life lessons not only through her words, but also through the life that she lived as a true servant of God, a faithful wife, a loving mom, a respectful daughter, and a loyal friend. She daily taught me godly characteristics such as self-discipline, hard work, and motivation, alongside lots of fun, laughter, singing, dancing, and just being silly. She taught me to live my life with integrity and excellence. I have always admired her quiet strength and her faith in God. Most of all, she has taught me the meaning of love.

I know many people say this about their moms, but I really believe that my mom is my greatest gift from God. So when I got the news that she was diagnosed with thyroid cancer, I was completely devastated. In denial and shock, I sat in my chair crying all night. How could this be happening? My mom had always been so full of life! She's always had more energy than me! On rare occasions (when I would actually wake up early in the morning), I would watch her exercise. Just watching her made me tired! So how could this be happening to *my mom*? I didn't understand, and like everyone else who has experienced this, thought, *Why her?*

What I didn't understand then was that God had a bigger plan. One of my favorite Scriptures is Jeremiah 29:11, "For I know the thoughts and plans I have for you, says the Lord, thoughts and plans for welfare and peace and not for evil, to give you hope in your final outcome." I don't know how many times I have found myself speaking those powerful, meaningful words over someone else's or my own life. Even if the plans aren't what we would have chosen, how much better our life might be if we surrender to God and allow him to use us for his glory? I started to see God's hand in all of this after my mom was diagnosed with thyroid cancer. What if my mom had to go through thyroid cancer to be a reflection of God's light, that same light that is so much a part of her own life, to help someone else going through the same experience? To her, everything she experienced was worth it if it helped even one person. God has had his hand over her the entire time. If he does that for her, he can do that for you. But that doesn't mean that he will have the same plan for you because we each have a unique purpose to fulfill in our life. If you surrender your life to God and allow him to use you, he will also give your life purpose and meaning.

My mom is the strongest woman I know, and even though cancer made her body weak, God stepped in and made her spirit strong. Rejoicing through the tears is exactly how it sounds. Through the tears and the struggle, you can still rejoice and find freedom because, no matter how severe your circumstances, you can always find hope in Jesus Christ. *Rejoicing through the Tears* is not only the title of my mom's book; it is the title of her life. I am truly blessed to be able to call Brenda George my mom. I pray that through this book there will be a divine transfer of faith, peace, and joy and that as you read this book, you will be encouraged to reach out beyond yourself into the loving arms of Jesus.

I am sure that my sister and brother, Bethany and Travis will say with me, "Her children rise up and call her blessed." (Proverbs 31:28)

With love,
Sarah, Bethany, and Travis

About the Author

Brenda George resides with her husband, Mark, in Marysville, Ohio. She is the mother of two grown daughters, Sarah and Bethany, a teenaged son, Travis, and grandmother to three adorable grandchildren, Savannah, Landon, and Jackson. Last but not least, she is the proud owner of her beloved Old English sheepdog, Maggie.

In high school, in her junior year, Brenda was listed in *Who's Who among American High School Students* for her achievement in the Miss Teenage America Pageant. Her poem "My Child, My Friend" was published in the Poetry Guild's anthology, *By the Light of the Moon*, in 1997.

Brenda is currently working on her next book and is planning speaking engagements to encourage other people who may be dealing with a cancer diagnosis or any other illness. She is also pursuing a career in nursing.

Since being diagnosed with thyroid cancer in 2007, Brenda wants to inspire people everywhere to never give up hope. They, too, can learn to rejoice through their tears and become stronger than they were before.

Acknowledgments

This book is dedicated to so many. First and foremost, it is written on behalf of those who have had a cancer diagnosis or any chronic illness, for that matter. This book is in honor of the millions of precious lives that have been cut short long before their time because of this dreaded disease, one of whom is my son-in-law's wonderful mother, Pamela Sue Franey, who lost her battle with colon cancer seventeen years ago.

This book is also dedicated to Kit Redman, who I knew for many years before either of us were diagnosed with cancer. You are such an inspiration to me as you have not let this disease change the person you are inside. You have always had that determination and sense of humor that so many of us know and love.

I would like to thank Kay Mitchell. I have always admired your wonderful contribution to your students at OSU and have been inspired from the many books you have written.

I would also like to thank the staff at Riverside Methodist Hospital in Columbus, Ohio, and to all of my doctors who were involved in my diagnosis and treatment. I have fully trusted you with my life and would recommend all of you to anyone. I was so fortunate to have the privilege to meet you and to receive such tremendous care.

And to my entire family. Where do I begin? Mere words are not adequate to express my love and thanks to each one of you. You have all played a part in my full recovery. You are what make each day count and make life a little sweeter each new day:

Mark, thank you for lending an ear to listen to the many excerpts I've read to you while writing this book. This has been a long two years, and I know I've been pretty moody many days. To my son-in-law, Chuck, thank you for your encouragement. I love your sense of humor. No matter what I'm going through, you usually make me laugh. To my daughter, Sarah, thank you for your faith in me as I wrote this book. You have been such fun to be around, and I love your determination in whatever you are doing. I appreciate your artistic touch in helping to design the cover for this book. To my other daughter, Bethany, thank you for helping me to learn Microsoft Word. You are the most patient person I know. To my son-in-law, Josh, thank you for getting my computer up and running so that I could write my book. I know you knew how important it was to me, and I'll always love you for it. I also know it has been hard for you because you lost your mom to cancer. To Travis, my son, I love you just because you're you. You always believed I could do it. To my granddaughter, Savannah, thanks sweetie, for the adorable artwork. You are so talented. To my little grandson, Landon, thank you for just being my sweetie pie. You have already inspired me to write my next book just as soon as this one is finished. To my other grandson, Jackson, I love you so much already. You are a fighter. I know God has something big for your life. To my mom, you've always been my biggest cheerleader. You never gave up hope. I guess that's just what a mother does.

Thanks so much for listening to me read the same stuff over and over again and acting like it was the first time you'd ever heard it. We cried together many times as I shared with you some of my deepest feelings. Thanks for seeing me through until the end. To my brother, Brent, and my nephews, Brian and Brandon, thank you for all of your loving words, encouragement, and the flowers and Starbucks drinks. I will never forget. I love you guys!

I would also like to thank all of you for the technical support. Although I've come a long way, I'm still not as computer savvy as I'd like to be. If it weren't for you, this book may not have come to completion, but still be tucked away in a drawer somewhere, screaming to get out.

A special person I want to mention is Brenna McGuire. Since we both went through thyroid cancer, we share a special bond. I love you, Brenna!

I will be forever grateful to each one of you for your unique way of contributing to the writing of this book. I love you all.

Most important, I want to thank my God. You gently put your hand in mine and led me each step of the way. Many times you carried me. You are my passion for living and my motivation behind this book. It's all about you.

Introduction

According to the latest statistics, thyroid cancer is on the rise. Whether you or someone you know has thyroid or another type of cancer or illness, *Rejoicing through the Tears* is written just for you.

A cancer diagnosis is very frightening. In fact, to most, it can be devastating. There are many types of cancer, and each case is unique. Many people beat this dreaded disease and go on to live full lives, but we know all too well that there are many who do not.

Regardless of your prognosis, my hope for you after reading *Rejoicing through the Tears* is to gain new insight into the comfort God can give you. You don't have to go through this experience alone. He will walk you through it, even carry you in his arms if need be. He will hold you and tend to your brokenness like a shepherd tending to his injured lamb. My prayer for you is to have a revelation of the vast love of Almighty God. Slip your hand in his, and let him lead you ever so gently through, whether it is to live out your life for many more years or to lead you to the other side. His plan is always perfect.

There can be life after a cancer diagnosis. It doesn't always have to mean the end. I am living proof. Although I have no guarantee of another day, I refuse to live one waking day worrying about it. Worry cannot add a single day to anyone's life

Philippians 4: 4-7 Rejoice in the Lord always; again, I say rejoice! Let all men know and perceive and recognize your unselfishness. The Lord is near. Do not fret or have any anxiety about anything, but in every circumstance and in everything, by prayer and petition, with thanksgiving, continue to make your wants known to God. And God's peace which transcends all understanding shall garrison and mount guard over your hearts and minds in Christ Jesus.

Matthew 6:34 So do not worry or be anxious about tomorrow, for tomorrow will have worries and anxieties of its own. Sufficient for each day is its own trouble. Therefore do not worry about tomorrow, for tomorrow will worry about itself. Each day has enough trouble of its own.

Rejoicing through the Tears is my personal journey through thyroid cancer and is written for the whole person, body, mind, and soul. I have added many uplifting Scripture passages that will ignite your faith. There is also a special section with my own personal tips to help you become fit, healthy, and to regain your vitality once again after having cancer. There are many little nuggets of wisdom to encourage you and to keep your attitude in line with God's word. I believe a healthy attitude is a key factor in recovering from any illness. Cancer leaves you with a fear of the unknown, but after reading *Rejoicing through the Tears*, you will be encouraged and receive renewed hope. While cancer is a frightening word, nothing is impossible with God. Psalm 118: 14 The Lord is my Strength and Song; and he has become my Salvation.

There is a section for caregivers of thyroid cancer patients and their families which contains resources and information about thyroid cancer, various websites, and cancer support groups. It is written with a bit of a sense of humor and a hint of patriotism, suggesting to the reader, the importance of love of God and country. I have always loved my country and still get cold chills when I hear the National Anthem and see our great American Flag waving so proudly. I believe our attitudes and beliefs about ourselves and others, as well as our faith in God and country are the driving force behind our actions, and they propel us forward to pursue optimum health and overall well being.

After reading *Rejoicing through the Tears,* you will know that no matter what happens, you can still rejoice with heartfelt joy from deep within that will spill over into all other areas of your life. You can learn to not only survive, but to thrive, to live with infectious passion and enthusiasm for life once again.

You can come through your wilderness journey of cancer as God will make a way for you like streams in the desert. Weeping may endure for a night, but joy will come in the morning. God will turn your mourning into dancing. You can say with me that our God is a good, good God!

Lamentations 3: 22-24 It is because of the Lord's mercy and loving-kindness that we are not consumed, because his compassions fail not. They are new every morning; great and abundant is Your stability and faithfulness. The Lord is my portion or share, says my living being; therefore will I hope in him and wait expectantly for him.

Isaiah: 43:19: Behold, I am doing a new thing! Now it springs forth; do you not perceive and know it and will you not give heed to it? I will even make a way in the wilderness and rivers in the desert.

Psalm 104; 33-34 I will sing to the Lord as long as I live; I will sing praise to my God while I have any being. May my meditation be sweet to him; as for me, I will rejoice in the Lord.

This book is about my personal experience with cancer, how I learned to cope with it and the knowledge I've gained from it. My desire is to offer hope, understanding, and encouragement to anyone who may be going through the same thing, and to encourage others to fight this dreaded disease and to never give up. I hope you will have gained words of comfort and sheer determination to keep on going, no matter what challenges you may be facing.

I have been given a good prognosis, and I realize that so many people haven't had a second chance. This book in no way intends to diminish anyone else's suffering.

This book is also not to take the place of your own medical doctor. It's simply my story of how I have learned, and am still learning, to cope with cancer.

If I can help even one person who may be going through what I have, this book will not have been written in vain. To anyone with a cancer diagnosis, I love you. I just want to give you a big hug and make it all better. I know the anguish and fear that I have experienced. Never give up hope. Let God embrace you in his awesome love and care for you at this time. Commit each day to him, and rest in him completely.

Disclaimer

This book is not to replace your medical doctor. It is intended for the sole purpose of use as a reference guide depending upon your particular case and your doctor's advice. Consult your doctor before following any suggestions in this book.

PART ONE

My Life before the Diagnosis

Before I was diagnosed with thyroid cancer, I was an ordinary person, just like you. I was working and enjoying my family. Not only was I busy with all of the regular day-to-day tasks, I had a lot of extra things going on at the same time. My oldest daughter, Sarah, was getting married, and I was caught up in all of the activities that go with being mother of the bride. My husband, Mark and I were also in the process of buying a car and looking forward to a long-awaited vacation. I had a full plate of varied activities, and I loved every minute of it. I thrive on activity! I know of no other way to say it: I just loved life!

Too often, when you hear the bad news that someone has cancer, it seems to define who they are and their destiny. It's easy to forget that they are real people, with families and jobs like everyone else. Even though they have cancer, they have hopes and dreams. Yes, dreams for a future.

They have a story to tell. A story of a time before cancer invaded their lives. I was unaware that I was even sick, not to mention that I was now a person with cancer. We are all on this journey called life, with no insight as to what lies ahead.

Chapter One

My Life before Cancer

This is a long story, so pour a cup of coffee.

I had a pleasant childhood, which I attribute to my parents. I was born in 1958, in Columbus, Ohio. I was always very busy, even as a small child. My mom said I went from walking to running almost overnight. After that, nothing could slow me down, and I have been that way ever since.

My dad owned his own bakery, and he was a wonderful baker and cook. I grew up enjoying any kind of fancy pastry I wanted. There was never a shortage of goodies at our house. It was every kid's dream; my sweet tooth was always satisfied. Year after year, Dad made and decorated all of our birthday cakes. My brother, Brent and I always looked forward to what new way Dad would decorate our cake, and he always came through, because each year they seemed to get better! We were so fortunate and the envy of all our friends. When I got married, he also made a beautiful wedding cake with a fountain in it. It was the talk of the town. As I got older, I'd often call him to get a recipe. No matter what recipe I needed, he always had it, although, it never tasted as good as it did when he made it. My mom is a great cook, also, but Dad had her spoiled. Almost every night when Mom came home from work, her dinner was piping hot, waiting for her on the table. Dad passed away several years ago, but I have so many great memories of him.

I have been blessed with a wonderful mom, also. When my younger brother, Brent and I were little, Mom was never too busy to let us know that we were more important to her than anything else. No matter what she was doing, she always stopped everything to give us her full attention. Nothing could ever replace those special moments that I remember as a child. One of my fondest memories was how Mom always took me shopping for a frilly Easter dress and bonnet—complete with white gloves and patent leather shoes. No matter how short my parents were on money at the time, they always managed to maintain special family traditions that were so important to us.

(This is one Sunday after church. Mom always made quite an issue about us all going to church and looking our best.)

Even these small family traditions blended together into beautiful, lasting childhood memories. As I look back with affection, I realize that those first impressionable years are what molded me into who I am today.

Brent is my only sibling, so it was just the two of us growing up. As adults, we are very close, but as kids, we teased each other constantly. We had our share of quarrels. I am two years older than Brent and I was the *tattletale*. He always said that he felt like he had two mothers while he was growing up. As I look back, I guess he was right, as much as I hate to admit it.

We grew up in a black and white ranch style house in the country. Our house was situated on one and a fourth acres. I remember my dad spending quite a bit of time outdoors in the summertime on the riding mower cutting our huge lawn. Across the road from our house was a field where cattle and horses roamed. Brent and I loved crossing the road in front of our house to reach in and pet the horses. I loved it! There wasn't much traffic on our country road. It was quiet and peaceful, but we were never bored. We always had plenty to do. Every summer, my parents planted a large garden. Brent and I had our own small gardens, and he was the one with the green thumb. I seemed to grow more weeds than anything. One summer, I decided to be a little artistic. I gathered as many rocks as I could find and put them all around my little garden. I painted them all beautiful colors. I didn't grow many vegetables that year, but my rocks sure were pretty.

Gardening wasn't all we did in the summer. We had great fun riding our minibike, although there were times that it was downright dangerous. I'll never forget the time I was riding the minibike, and I hit a bump. I did a cartwheel over the handlebars—like a stunt man—before coming to a sudden halt. I can still almost feel the impact. I'm not sure what hurt the most; the thud I felt after hitting the bump, or the shock I experienced at the deafening silence when it was all over. I was quite a tomboy growing up, and I loved to ride my bicycle for miles. I loved putting my puppy in the basket, and off we would go.

Even though I loved riding my bicycle on country roads, my big dream as a little girl was to own a pony. On my twelfth birthday, my parents fulfilled that dream and surprised me with a beautiful pony named "Blackie." I spent as much time as I could out in the field riding him. One afternoon while I was riding Blackie, he brushed against the electric fence. The shock startled him so much that he threw me off and began running. I ended up with a broken leg and had to spend the entire summer in a cast. The accident ended that summer's fun.

When I was in third grade, I had a Sunday school teacher I will never forget. Mrs. McPherson taught me so much about the Bible, life, and love. She not only taught it, she lived it. And she made a huge impact on my life.

(This is my grandparents' wonderful house. If you look closely, you will see Grandma and Grandpa standing on their wraparound porch.)

My grandparents were also a special part of my life. They lived in a small town that bustled with activity. There were many sights and sounds that I learned to appreciate more with every summer spent with them. Their large home was always so inviting. It was a two story white house with a wraparound porch, but it was so much more than a house. It was a home. There was just no place on earth quite like my grandparents' house. Each day I eagerly awaited to hear the church bells ring at noon. The railroad tracks were across the street from their house. The once loud, annoying sound of the slow-moving trains, chugging tiredly down the tracks became a welcome sound that I soon learned to look forward to. My grandparents' house sat beside the fire station. Every time there was a fire or a police call, the deafening sirens would jolt me out of my seat. Since we were next door to the fire station, I became best friends with all the firemen. I knew every one of them and hung out quite a bit with them. I actually became their mascot and got to ride in the big, red, fire truck with them in all the local parades. Those were the good old days. There was always something to do, and it always spelled fun!

Grandma used to send me to the dime store to shop for those special treats that she knew I loved. She used to place her warm, loving hands over mine as she slipped a brand-new dollar bill in my small hands. You could buy quite a bit for a dollar those days. On the way to the dime store, I passed the bakery, where the smell of freshly baked brownies always beckoned me to stop in.

My favorite place to go when visiting my grandparents was the old school playground that had been there for years. The tall metal slide had a uniqueness all of its own. As my small legs climbed each step, getting closer to the top, I couldn't wait for the slippery ride straight back down. I would land in a clump of gritty sand at the bottom. As the sand trickled through my toes, I would race delightedly to the top of the ladder for another thrilling ride. I played hard, and thoroughly enjoyed myself many afternoons in that small Newcomerstown, Ohio community. Many memories were made there while visiting my grandparents' house.

Eventually, sheer exhaustion would set in, and I would trudge down the narrow alley leading back to my grandparents' large white house. At last, I would see Grandpa's old, white barn that was so well kept. Inside the barn, Grandpa had a refrigerator stocked full of icy cold soda in every flavor a kid could want.

Grandpa was a perfectionist about his barn and yard. Everything manifested neatness. His vegetable garden had many plants just ripe for the picking: green beans; sweet corn; strawberries; rhubarb; large, unblemished russet potatoes; and cucumbers, to name a few. Most of all, I loved his enormous Big Boy tomatoes, which were juicy—enough to tempt the finickiest palate.

Grandma had a beautiful flower garden, every bit as adorning as Grandpa's vegetable garden. She had every imaginable flower and shrub, including lilac bushes, roses, peonies, hydrangeas, and many other fragrant and colorful plants. At the beginning of every summer, her garden almost looked as if God had taken a giant paintbrush and painted a masterpiece, just for our pleasure.

Grandma and Grandpa's house was quite large with spacious rooms all painted in a soft, fresh white. The coziest room by far was Grandma's kitchen. As I awoke each morning, a trail of tempting smells invited me to breakfast. I would hear Grandma clamoring about and the clanging of pots and pans as she was lovingly preparing everyone's breakfast with a smile. You could smell fresh eggs frying, toast as it popped up in the toaster, crunchy bacon as it sizzled, and my favorite: the aroma of hot coffee brewing.

After breakfast, we would all gather around and Grandma would play her piano for us. She was extremely talented. She played in a jazz band in her younger years. She could almost make the keys dance by themselves.

In the evening when the sun began to set and the air was crisp, we would grab a can of soda pop and sit on the front porch. We would gaze at the busy town until it quieted at last. We were lulled to sleep by the back-and-forth motion of the porch swing.

My most cherished moment of all was Grandma's warm smile and that loving sparkle in her eyes. Hers was another precious life lost to cancer, as she died of Melanoma, a form of skin cancer. Even though, they are both gone now, I will always cherish the memories of summers spent with them. I always get a warm feeling as I reflect over those days gone by.

The shift into my teen years was a smooth transition. I took baton and dancing lessons until I graduated from high school and absolutely loved it. Everything I did revolved around baton and dancing. One year in junior high, I led our baton group in the Fourth of July parade in our local town. We were called the Plain City Sugarplums. Wherever there was a dance recital, I was in it. I danced my way right through high school.

(This is me in my baton uniform.)

I took an office course in high school, which I didn't enjoy very much. Our class picked me to do the talent segment at our national office convention, because everyone knew that I could dance much better than I could type.

I entered the Miss Teenage America Pageant and was picked as a semifinalist in my junior year of high school and was listed in *Who's Who among American High School Students*.

Meanwhile, all of my friends were learning to drive. I took Drivers Ed, and finally got my driver's license when I was sixteen years old. Don't ask me how since for me learning to drive was quite an experience. For starters, I had an instructor who was also the high school football coach. For all he taught me, he should have stayed on the football field, which was where his mind was anyway. He had to have nerves of steel to get into the car with any of us behind the wheel.

The hardest part of all for me was parking. We tried everything. My dad took me to the park and set up parking cones for practice. That didn't work. My driving instructor grew very impatient with me. He spent an entire morning picking up the cones, as each time I knocked them all down.

My friend, Joanna, who was in my Driver's Ed class, almost drove us into a concrete bridge because a bird flew in front of the car. Every time it was my turn to drive, my instructor would get very upset with me. He would say, "You're going to have to start stopping at these stop signs!" I always had a hard time judging traffic lights. I would get going, and then realize that I had to stop. It's a miracle we didn't all have to wear neck braces for the remaining school year. For safety's sake, maybe we should have, just as a precaution.

No matter how hard I tried, I failed my driver's test, but the day finally came to take my driver's test for the second time, and do you know what? I passed!

My very first car was really neat, which my parents bought from an elderly couple for fifty dollars. Can you imagine that? That's unheard of these days. It was a 1951 Buick Special and it was special alright. I was never as proud of anything in my life as I was that car. It was loaded with many gadgets. It even came with a set of pliers to turn the windshield wipers on and off. And if you think that was great, the car could somehow be started without a key for some unknown reason. The only problem with that was that I had to worry that someone might steal it. "Oh well. You can't have everything," I told myself. Fixing it would have cost more than the car, itself. The shocks were so bad that the car hopped like a rabbit everywhere I went. It was okay, though, because it saved me lots of money on roller coaster rides in the end. I can laugh now because it's in the past, and I've moved on to new and better cars. Seriously speaking, that was one of my most trying times growing up. But I got through it, although I probably caused my parents to age before their time.

After I graduated from high school, I worked at an insurance company as a typist and hated it because I hated sitting still all day long. I needed something that required action. That job just wasn't for me.

After that, I became a nurse's assistant at our local hospital, where I worked for three years and loved it. I enjoyed helping people. It was so rewarding. I then trained to become an EMT technician and applied to nursing school. In the meantime, I met my soon-to-be husband, Mark, which changed my plans completely. We fell in love and got married in 1980 when I was 23 years old and have been married for thirty years.

(Mark and I had been miniature golfing at Traverse City Michigan)

How cool is that? After we were married two months, I found out that I was expecting our first child, Sarah. Five years later, Bethany came along, and five years after that, Travis was born.

I loved being a wife and mother more than life itself and finally realized the meaning of true happiness. I also loved taking care of my house and everything that went along with it, especially decorating. In 1987, Mark and I bought our first home and did all the things that new homeowners do like planting grass seed numerous times and all of the other aspects that go with owning a home.

When the kids were little, I was home with them as much as possible. I started a small cleaning business, but my kids were my first priority, so I worked everything around them. I took all three of them everywhere I went. You've probably heard of the movie, *Three Men and a Baby;* well, we were *Three Kids and a Mom.* I took them to every house that I cleaned; I don't know how I did it, but I managed. The people I worked for would come home from work, and their house would look like a day care center. I'd have the playpen set up for the baby, and he would be hanging from the doorway in his airplane swing. Bottles, bibs, and jars of baby food were scattered all over the kitchen counters, the diaper bag was plopped on the couch, and the toys littered the floor." Let me tell you! I worked for some very patient people, who were all just like family to me. By the time I packed up everything and left their houses, everything sparkled and shined as if the kids had never been there.

I always loved being busy, and busy we were. Grocery shopping with all three kids was more than treacherous. The shopping carts were boring back then. These days, there are too many choices. You can choose between one with an infant seat, one with three seats, or one that looks like a car. You know you're a mother when you are pushing a grocery cart the size of a minivan. I guess that's a sign that you have a lot of kids. I have always said that I played the game of *Life* too much when I was a child, because my car was always full of kids, and that still hasn't changed. Now, it's my grandchildren that I'm enjoying, and I wouldn't have it any other way!

(Sarah and Bethany sharing a soda and a sisterly moment)

(Those toothless smiles are priceless!)

Kids have a way of keeping you busier than you ever thought possible, and as they got older, we got busier and busier. Sarah was on the swim team. We spent many mornings at the pool and many evenings at various swim meets. She, my artistic one, also loved art and entered many contests in school. I'll never forget the night she told me about her huge science project that was due the next day, which she had forgotten all about. Needless to say, we did some quick cramming, staying up all night to work on it. She had to type up a report, and we didn't have a computer back then. We had one of those old fashioned typewriters with the messy ribbons. That was one night that I will never forget. Even then, I paused for a moment, in brief sadness, because I knew in just a short time, it would fade away into a memory.

Bethany played softball and took horseback riding lessons. She was my accident prone one, so, when we weren't running to softball games, we were visiting the emergency room quite regularly. She was quite a tomboy. I can still see her playing hockey in front of our house wearing rollerblades.

Travis was a typical boy who never stood still for longer than a minute at a time. He played almost every sport known to man, and Mom, and was on the school golf team in his eighth grade year of junior high school. I was so proud of him. I'll never forget the time I went golfing with him and his buddies. We rented a cart, but I couldn't hit my ball far enough to ride anywhere. I did a lot of walking that day all by myself.

They were all on the speed skating team for a short while. Between the many practices and running them and their friends to and from one another's houses, my kids were growing up right before my eyes. But I was so busy with them that their growing up was like a sneak attack. There were times I felt as though I was suffering a temporary case of insanity, but I guess I'd just been extremely preoccupied for quite a long time. Raising kids can definitely wear you out and make you question the fact of having any brain cells left to function properly. When the kids were little, I took a course for writing children's books and published a poem in the anthology, *By the Light of the Moon*, titled "My Child, My Friend." Sarah, Bethany, and Travis were definitely my inspiration.

What our parents fail to teach us, we can be sure that our children will. They teach us so much about life, love, and definitely patience. Even when times were chaotic, I was able to find humor in the midst of everyday life. Life goes on, and kids grow up like mine have done. It wasn't always easy, especially when they were learning to drive. Now I know what my parents went through. When Sarah learned to drive, I almost had to be sedated to get into the passenger side of the car. I'd never felt so out of control in my life.

I never thought the day would come, but now I can look back and honestly say, *"We made it!"* We had a few rocky times along the way, one of them being when Sarah became an unwed mother. I was very upset, to say the least, but we loved her right through it anyway. Now I can't imagine a single day without my granddaughter, Savannah. She is a true blessing in all of our lives. I, now, have two little grandsons, Landon, and baby Jackson. I'll tell you more about them in a later chapter.

It may sound cliché, but it is true. I remember hearing so many older, (or so I thought at the time), people tell me to enjoy my kids when they were little, because "These are the best days of your life", they would say. I used to think they were crazy. How could this be the best time in a mother's life? There's too much work to do, like laundry, diapers, tantrums, ballgames, swimming lessons . . . . You know what I mean if you're a mother. I remember feeling, on some days, that I was on a treadmill, running at full pace and the only way to get off was to fall off in sheer exhaustion. Now, as I reflect back on those days, I miss them. I miss those carefree days spent at the pool, too. I even miss those school conferences. I didn't realize that I would miss them, but it's true. They really were the best days of my life!

I heard the story of a man who was having a difficult time in his life. He was divorced, had two young sons, and was going through some financial problems. He had a good job and worked very long, hard hours. No matter how hard he worked, he just couldn't make ends meet.

He loved his two boys more than life itself, always putting their needs above his own. He sacrificed so much just to take care of them, yet he only got to see them every other weekend. One weekend, he was more sad and discouraged than usual and was about at the end of his rope. It seemed like no matter how hard he tried, nothing seemed to go right.

That particular weekend happened to be Fathers Day, and it wasn't his weekend to see the boys. *It was probably good anyway,* he thought, since he was out of groceries. Meanwhile, the boys had a plan of their own. Since it was Fathers Day, they asked their mom to take them for a surprise visit to see their dad, as they wanted to serve him breakfast in bed. They searched his bare cupboards, and way back in the corner, there was one muffin left that he didn't know was there. They surprised him with the last muffin. All of his love and sacrifice paid off, because his sons took that love he had bestowed on them and gave it back to him. They gave him so much more than a muffin that Fathers Day morning. They gave him renewed hope and the will to go on.

As you can probably tell by now, I've always been a very family-oriented person. My husband, children, grandchildren, as well as my mother, brother and nephews are my life. I strongly believe in the family unit, especially in today's society. More than ever, we need strong families.

Our family has the same ups and downs as any other family, but when we all get together, there's a lot of noise, laughter, and, of course, food. We're always doing something on the crazy side, and it's usually my idea. One year, we had a murder mystery dinner on Friday the thirteenth. We had Italian cuisine with Death by Chocolate cake for dessert, which just seemed fitting. We also had a Hawaiian luau in our backyard several years ago, complete with grass skirts and Hawaiian music.

We just like to have fun and hang out together, and whatever we do doesn't have to be elaborate. One winter, we went snow tubing. That was my first and last adventure doing anything that dangerous. I'm not ashamed to admit that I'm entirely too old for such daring escapades. I felt like I was going five hundred miles an hour down a huge hill *backward* on a solid sheet of ice. I made a promise to God and to myself that if I made it to the bottom of the hill with my entire body still intact, I'd never try anything like that again. As I look back, I don't think cancer was any more dangerous.

This is my story before cancer and who I still am today. I was forty-nine when I was diagnosed with thyroid cancer and was just starting to kick back a bit, thinking my kids were almost raised. I thought that I would have more time to finally do some of the things that I'd been too busy to do for so long like just relax. I am now fifty-three. I don't know how it's possible, as I'm not sure where all the years have gone. I'm not looking forward to getting older, but when I consider the alternative, its fine with me. I'm just thankful to be here. Life can be a frightening journey, even without cancer, when you go it all alone. I compare it to being blindfolded and sent on a long trip without a map or a destination. Sometimes when I stop for just a moment and listen to that still small voice, I hear Jesus say, ever so gently, "Just trust me. Put your hand in mine. I'll show you great and mighty things. You're in for the time of your life!"

By now, you are probably wondering what any of this has to do with cancer. I'm glad you asked. There are times this book may pull at your heartstrings. There will be times when you will laugh, and other times, you might cry, especially when you think of your own life and special memories. I believe there is healing in our laughter as well as our tears.

Before my cancer diagnosis, I had always been blessed with good health. As I'm one of those health nuts, I drive everyone else crazy about it also. My heartfelt advice to everyone I know is to eat healthy and exercise. I love being active. There are never enough hours in a day for me. Life is a wonderful journey to celebrate from every bird that sings in the morning to every sun that sets in the evening. I just love life.

Scripture:

Psalm 16:11
You will show me the path of life; in Your presence is fullness of joy, at Your right hand there are pleasures forevermore.

Chapter Two

The Wedding

During the spring of 2007, life was good. In fact, it was great! We were planning Sarah's wedding in April of that year. She was our first child to leave home, so it was quite an emotional experience.

Anyone who has ever planned a wedding knows exactly what I'm talking about. I was emotionally and physically drained from the many sleepless nights because of all the deadlines that had to be met. It was a lot of hard work, but in a good way. After all, I was *Mother of the Bride!* It was exhausting, but I was having the time of my life.

During all the chaos, I watched the movie *Father of the Bride* over and over. At first I laughed, and then I cried. I felt sorry for my poor husband, as he was the one upon whom I took out all of my frustrations. I wasn't much fun to live with. I was even more emotional than Sarah.

Amidst all of the busyness, I managed to fit in an appointment for my annual checkup, where my doctor noticed that my neck was swollen and wanted me to see a specialist to rule out anything serious. I told him how busy things were, but reassured him that I'd do it the first thing after the wedding. I was almost positive there was nothing to be concerned about.

There was still so much to be done. The lists were endless, and our time was running out; there were not enough hours in a day. We still needed to:

- Get the cake.
- Talk to the photographer.
- Plan the music.
- Get the bridesmaids' dresses, flower girl dresses, and my Mother of the Bride dress.
- Have the men fitted for their tuxedos.
- Talk to the caterer.
- Plan the reception.
- Talk to the DJ.
- Go to Sarah's final wedding-gown fitting.
- Talk to the minister.
- Go to the bridal showers.

Everything was moving so fast. This time in my life was hectic, not to mention expensive, but that didn't matter. I wanted nothing but the best for my baby.

Before I knew it, the big day was upon us. The weather couldn't have been more beautiful. When we arrived at the church, it was everything I could have hoped for. All of the hard work and expense was worth it. All that mattered was that this was the most important day of my daughter's life, and I was so happy to be a part of it.

The horse and carriage were waiting in front of the church to take the newly married couple on their first romantic ride together.

As I entered the church, it was like a glimpse of heaven. The scent of spring flowers lingered everywhere. Tall candelabras with softly glowing candles graced the altar. The aisles were adorned with topiaries, and elegant bows draped the church pews as they gracefully flowed to the floor. There was a hush before the organ music started playing in the background. I took a deep breath, a final sigh of relief, and tears started streaming down my face. It seemed like only yesterday that I was the one walking down the aisle.

Memories of Sarah's childhood started flashing through my mind. I remembered so well the posters covering her bedroom walls and all of the pictures of her friends. I remember the boy she had her first crush on. Time stood still as I could almost hear her small voice in the distance calling her daddy to push her on the swing. Then, there was that first bicycle ride without training wheels as I witnessed that proud look on her face when she realized that she was riding all on her own. One lasting memory that will forever be in my heart was the first day of school when that big, yellow school bus stopped in front of our house, and my little girl left for the first time. I knew then that my time with her would be brief, and that time never stands still. My first encounter with the realization that she was growing up too fast was the same sadness I was feeling on her wedding day. Letting go is a hard lesson to learn.

I snapped back to reality when the bridal march began. As mother of the bride, I was prompted to stand first. When I turned around, there she was in her beautiful wedding gown with her dad at her side. Her tiara glistened more with each step she took. She had never looked more beautiful. Even though, I was with her at her final gown fitting, there was something different about her today. She was glowing. As our eyes met, my heart met hers, and my tears of sadness turned to tears of joy. She was so happy, and I was rejoicing with her.

I started thinking about how my other children were growing up as well. It wouldn't be long before I would be attending their weddings. Bethany, Sarah's maid of honor, was just as beautiful as Sarah, and Travis was an usher. When did he grow up and become so handsome? Savannah was a flower girl and was just adorable. I remember when Sarah, Bethany, and Travis were at the tender age of three. Just a short time ago, I was rocking them all on my knee. Where had all the time gone? Life goes so fast!

Scripture:

So teach us to number our days that we may get a heart of wisdom.

Psalm 90:12

Mark and Sarah on her wedding day.
(A proud papa!)

(Reflecting on the past few months leading up to this moment.)

Chapter Three

The First Doctor Visit

After the wedding, things started returning to normal again. There was a letdown after all of the excitement, and I was tired, but it felt good to relax.

A couple of weeks later, I made an appointment with the specialist to have my neck checked. My doctor wanted me to have an MRI, which I thought was a waste of time and money, but I followed doctor's orders anyway.

I worked on the day that the MRI was scheduled. I didn't know what to expect, but I assumed there would be nothing to it. I thought I'd just run in after work, get it over with, and that would be the end of it.

The nurse told me that I needed to lie very still for about an hour. She placed a bar across my neck and turned on music to help me relax. She handed me a call button in case I needed her and then left the room. I didn't realize that I was so claustrophobic. After a few minutes, I couldn't stand it any longer and told the nurse that I couldn't go through with it. I thought the MRI was unnecessary because I felt just fine, so I decided to forget the entire thing.

A couple of weeks went by and my doctor had another plan. He wanted me to try it again, but this time, he made sure that I was asleep so that I was unaware of what was going on. That was the only way that I would have agreed to it.

The results came back a week later: I had seven nodules on my thyroid gland. I might not be here today if I hadn't had that MRI. The bump on my neck turned out to be a blessing in disguise.

When I found out the results, I was frightened. My voice had been hoarse for awhile, and I had some difficulty swallowing. I was also more tired than usual, but I thought it was just because of all of the stress from the wedding.

A week later, my doctor wanted me to have an ultrasound done on the nodules. He promised that it was a painless procedure, but I was still anxious about it.

This is where my nightmare began, in the spring, and continued until Christmas. When I first started going to the doctor, the offices had vases of spring flowers in their waiting rooms. As time went on, and I went from one doctor visit to the next, the spring flowers were replaced by Christmas decorations and poinsettias. When you've had cancer, you notice little things like that; things that most people don't even think about.

It seemed like it would never end; I had an eerie feeling that it was only the beginning.

Scripture:

Do not let your hearts be troubled. You believe in and adhere to and trust in and rely on God; believe in and adhere to and trust in and rely also on me. Peace I leave with you; My peace I now give and bequeath to you. Not as the world gives do I give to you. Do not let your hearts be troubled, neither let them be afraid.

John 14:1, 27

Chapter Four

The Vacation

After the ultrasound, I stayed as busy as possible, trying not to worry. Mark and I bought a new Mazda Miata convertible. I had wanted a car like that all my life, and one with two seats seemed appropriate for the empty-nest syndrome that I was beginning to experience, hence my driving a sports car at my age. Even though I still had two kids at home, I knew it wouldn't be long until they would have plans of their own. I was feeling a bit weepy those days. I guess that just goes with the territory of being a mother.

No matter how bad things seemed, riding around in that sports car with the top down and my hair blowing in the wind made all of my worries disappear, even if it was only temporary.

We took our vacation that summer to our favorite family destination, my favorite place in the world, Mackinac Island, Michigan. That beautiful island is the epitome of peace and is a little bit of heaven on earth where everything seems to stand still. For the last twenty years, that is where our family has vacationed to get away from it all. When the kids were teenagers, it was nice to whisk them away and have them all to ourselves for awhile. That was not always easy during the barrage of teen frenzy that goes on at that age.

I can attempt to describe the island to you, but the only way to get the feel of the place is to go yourself. You will, then, know why I feel so fortunate to have discovered such a unique place, and why I love it so much!

It has an authentic Victorian image. There are between 500 and 600 permanent residents that reside there year round who are warm and friendly with the tourists. If you are into history, you need to go, because it abounds there.

Throughout the years, many different Indian tribes camped on the island's shores, with one of the largest tribes being the Chippewa tribe. The fur industry was an important part of history on the island. Fort Mackinac, a beautifully restored military post was originally built by the British, because they were concerned about American attack on Fort Michilimackinac during the Revolutionary War. It was built on a steep hill overlooking the harbor. In 1875, Congress proclaimed most of Mackinac Island to be our second national park, because of its rich history, natural beauty and unique atmosphere. Mackinac Island is the home of the well-known Grand Hotel. In 1979, the movie *Somewhere in Time* was filmed there starring Christopher Reeves and Jane Seymour.

There are many weddings that take place on the island, because of its romantic atmosphere. And every July, people from all over the world come to compete in the annual yacht races held there.

The famous Mackinac Bridge is one of the main attractions. As you approach the bridge at night, you can see the lights from miles away. The bridge connects the upper and lower peninsulas of Michigan—the north end is St. Ignace, and the south end is

Mackinac City. It is five miles across. One day every year, pedestrians are allowed to walk across the bridge. It is known as the "Labor Day Bridge Walk." The walkers are led by the Governor of Michigan. It is an important annual event.

There are two ways to get to the island, from Mackinac City or St. Ignace. There is a small airport where you can fly to the island, but the most popular way is to take the ferry boat.

As you are approaching the island, from a distance, it seems void of any activity, but the closer you get, all of the houses and the Grand Hotel come into full view. It is, then, that you realize what a busy place it is with an agenda all of its own. It's set apart from the real world, as we know it, but it bustles with activity. Once you enter the harbor, jammed with boats, and see the many visitors entering or leaving the island, you will be mesmerized as you are caught up in the moment of this special place that takes you back in time. Everything is busy and moving, but at an incredibly unhurried pace. At that moment, all of your cares seem to disappear and you suddenly feel that this magical island will always be a part of you.

There are no cars on Mackinac Island. The modes of transportation are bicycle, horse, and, of course, foot. It has a soothing tranquility that adds to the special charm. Amidst the tranquility are distinct sounds that make the island what it is. You can hear the clip-clop of horse's feet as they casually walk down Main Street without a care in the world. Off in the distance, you can hear the boats tooting their horns as they near the ferry docks. Overhead, sea gulls are screeching and flapping their wings and soaring above the water as the waves rush in and crash up against the giant, white rocks along the shore.

There is every type of bicycle imaginable. For those of us who can't live without our cars, when you get to Mackinac Island, you can't live without your bicycle. Everything is so much simpler and laid back on Mackinac Island, which is why I love it so much. Plus, I love fudge, and fudge shops are everywhere. The mere smell of it makes my mouth water. The tourists are called "fudgies" by the islanders, because not many people can leave Mackinac Island without taking some fudge with them.

The annual Lilac Festival is held every June, and is one of our nation's top one hundred tourist attractions. The lilacs have full blooms in shades of lavender and white. Hotels and bed and breakfasts are plentiful along Main Street and throughout the island. They all have hanging baskets full of colorful flowers on their balconies, where it's fun to sit back and watch the hustle and bustle of activities that take place all day long.

Mackinac Island is also known for its spacious mansions, including the Governor's summer residence, and its breathtaking views. There are several peaks that you can climb to the top and look out over the water and the golf courses. The Grand Hotel golf course is named "The Jewel."

People love to go to Marquette Park to relax or to read a good book. Some of them you find spending a carefree afternoon tumbling on the lawn with their children. The beautifully landscaped lawns are a popular picnic spot with gorgeous flowers, trees and lilac bushes, with a playground for young children. No matter what you like to do, you will always feel a gentle breeze on your face as the sailboats sail in the distance and you hear the echo of children's laughter.

We love to bike ride the island's eight-mile perimeter along the water, which is as blue as the ocean.

There are many aspects of island life that I love, but the one that stands out, foremost, in my mind are the American flags that stand tall in everyone's front lawn. They wave as the wind furiously whips them back and forth, announcing to the world that this is my country, and I'm proud of it!

Have I convinced you to visit Mackinac Island? Take it from me, you won't be disappointed. Although it's part of the world we live in, it feels so far away from the cares of everyday life as we know it. I get a sense of peace, and my world is suddenly calmed by just the mention of it. I am captivated by every inch of this amazing island. It's definitely a land of enchantment.

Our vacation that year started out great. The weather was beautiful. My mom went with Mark and I and the kids. Sarah's husband, Chuck, stayed behind because he had to work. We drove the scenic route along the water and took our time exploring every detail along the way. The scenery was awesome. We stopped at a beautiful beach for a picnic and walked in the sand in our bare feet. Once on the island, Bethany and Travis took Savannah on a bike ride. One of the first things I did after checking into our hotel was to stop and buy some of that creamy fudge. I could hear it calling my name the first moment my feet landed on the island. There was something different about it that year, though. Why was it so hard to swallow? Did they use a different recipe? I had never noticed it before. Mark stayed in the hotel room to relax and read, and Mom, Sarah and I did what most women do. We shopped. I bought Mom an elegant hat in a quaint little shop. She has always been a hat lover. The kids all loved taking her picture throughout the trip of Grandma in her hat. I bought a small lilac bush to take home to plant in my backyard, hoping I could take home with me, just a small piece of the island. I babied that plant through the entire vacation. I even named it Lila. Regretfully, Lila didn't make it home alive. As sad as I was, it became our family joke.

We were having so much fun. It was another family memory that I would always treasure. In the early mornings, Mark and Travis liked to hit the golf course, and in the evenings it was refreshing to put my feet up and sit back in my Adirondack chair with the view of the Mackinac Bridge. On my most hectic of days, I love to hold onto that memory. It felt great to unwind, feeling that peaceful calm that I had been yearning for during the last few hectic months.

Little did we all know, that peace was about to be shattered. After we had been on Mackinac Island a few short days, the doctor's office called saying that the ultrasound didn't look good and that I needed further testing. They wanted me to have a biopsy as soon as we returned home from vacation.

Scripture:

From the end of the earth will I cry to you, when my heart is overwhelmed and fainting; lead me to the rock that is higher than I.

Psalm 61:2

(The Mackinac Bridge)

(If you look closely, you will see the American flag on top of the Grand Hotel)

(This is a carriage tour on Mackinac Island. This picture was taken in front of St. Anne's Catholic Church, amidst the many people on bicycles that day.)

Chapter Five

The Diagnosis

After we returned home from Mackinac Island, I reluctantly made an appointment for the biopsy. I still did not think there was anything to be concerned about, because I felt too good. Sick people were the ones who had something wrong, I thought.

I went to the hospital bright and early the next Monday morning, following my return home from vacation for a fine-needle biopsy in my neck. I was dragging my feet all the way to the hospital. I just couldn't stand to hear any more bad news. As I was lying flat on my back on the table, the tears rolled down both sides of my face and dripped onto the examination table. I couldn't explain it, but somewhere deep down inside, I sensed the worst.

The doctor doing the biopsy told me that thyroid nodules are fairly common. Ninety-five percent of them are benign, leaving only five percent as malignant. That was reassuring to hear.

While your medical history, examination by a physician, lab tests, and ultrasound are important, the only test that can distinguish whether thyroid nodules are benign or malignant is through a fine-needle biopsy. After numbing the area, the doctor sticks a very fine needle into the nodules to remove cells for microscopic examination, which are sent to pathology. A bandage is put on your neck, and you are sent home.

The biopsy wasn't too painful, but I would describe it as uncomfortable. Every day of the rest of that week seemed to be an eternity as I waited for that phone call with the biopsy results. Finally, the nurse called three days later. She hesitated for a few minutes on the other end of the line before she reluctantly said that it was urgent that I make an appointment as soon as possible. What more can I say except that it was a *long weekend*!

Monday finally rolled around. I was in a daze as I walked into the doctor's office early that morning. The doctor sat down in his chair and looked me straight in the eye with apprehension. If I didn't know better, I would have sworn I saw a single tear in his eye when he gave me the news that I was dreading to hear with all my heart—that I had papillary thyroid cancer—but my eyes were so welled up with tears, I wasn't sure,

I was not prepared to hear those heart-wrenching words that would pierce my heart forever. They cut like a knife. It was the worst shock of my life, and I was completely numb inside. The true meaning of those words hadn't sunk in yet. They were just too final.

I came out of the doctor's office and into the waiting room where my mom was waiting for me. I tried to smile, but it was forced. I wanted to act like everything was normal for as long as I could and put off telling her the news that had just turned my own world upside down. As we walked out of the hospital, my legs felt like lead. Each step became more impossible.

Finally, when I fell into my car that was it. There was no holding back. I completely broke down. The tears started and went on for at least a week, almost nonstop. I remember eating my bowl of cereal that next morning before work and crying the entire time. I didn't know my body was capable of producing so many tears. Finally, there were no more tears left to cry. But I still felt completely hopeless.

Papillary thyroid cancer is a very treatable kind of cancer. The prognosis is usually good if it is caught in time, which it usually is, and receives the proper treatment. There are many more cases being diagnosed each year, mainly because technology is now so much more advanced. If mine hadn't been diagnosed when it was, it would have probably become terminal.

I was thankful that the outlook was encouraging, but I didn't like hearing anyone pass it off as the *good* cancer. There is no *good* cancer. Cancer can kill. It may be slow, depending on what type it is and the stage it's in, but left untreated, death is almost inevitable. The C word is one that nobody ever wants to hear. That very word meant death to me.

If I was fortunate enough to survive, my life would be forever changed and would require lifelong monitoring.

Scripture:

God is our Refuge and Strength, a very present and well-proved help in trouble.

Psalm 46:1

Part Two

My Experience with Thyroid Cancer

This section is about my experience with thyroid cancer, including the surgery and radiation, and how I learned to deal with it emotionally as well as physically.

I had to come to grips with the realization that I had cancer and learn to face the diagnosis head on. There was no way to avoid it. Cancer was there, the real deal, staring me in the face, like it or not.

During this part of my life, the tears were plentiful as there was not much to rejoice about. I was in my own dark valley that became a rigorous journey through the wilderness, a barren time in my life that I could only describe as the Midnight Hour. In this time of great brokenness, I felt completely alone.

As you will see, this was when and where my emotional and spiritual growth began. I had to go through the valley to get to the mountaintop. Only then did I discover true rejoicing.

Chapter Six

Life Goes On . . . Or Does It?

No one is ever prepared for a cancer diagnosis. I was in total shock as were my family and friends. After all, I was in the prime of my life. This was all just a bad dream, right? Wrong. Oh, how wrong.

Unless you're the one going through it, you could never know the impact that one word—cancer—has upon your life, physically as well as emotionally. *How could this be happening to me? I have always taken good care of myself and have tried to do everything right . . . . I'm still young . . . . I'm too busy for this intrusion . . . . This isn't fair,* circled through my mind over and over. There were days when I just stared into space. As hard as I tried to argue it away and make some kind of sense of it all, I just couldn't. I cried, and I cried. I retreated into my own little world and closed the door behind me. I put up an invisible wall, stayed within its boundaries, and didn't let anyone in to invade my territory.

I felt the love of my family and friends around me, but this was my problem and my life. I had never felt so alone. There was nothing anyone else could do to help me or to take the cancer away. My doctors were all wonderful, but they were used to seeing sick people every day. It was their job. They were also used to seeing people die. I wanted to scream at the top of my lungs, "Help Me!" But instead, I withdrew from the world.

I was so afraid. I started reading my Bible and praying more than I ever had in my life for I knew that I needed to trust in God. I remembered being a child in Mrs. McPherson's Sunday school class. I began to think of all the wonderful things she taught me and her calm but simple faith in the loving God that she knew so well. She was an older lady, and I admired her so much. She had such wisdom. She taught me how to come to God as a little child and to simply trust him and to read the bible and to BELIEVE it. She taught me kindness and about the amazing love of God, and that no matter where I was or what I was ever going through, it was never too hard for him to handle. I remembered those old hymns we sang at vacation bible school, *What a Friend We Have in Jesus, the Old Rugged Cross, Trust and Obey*, and my favorite, *I come to the Garden Alone*. I knew that he was going to take care of me, no matter what happened, and that he had everything under control. He had a plan for my life before I had ever been born, and his plan was far greater than mine.

After awhile, I got angry. I wasn't mad at God, but my faith wasn't that strong at the beginning. I was still holding onto my doubts and fears, rather than trusting God completely. I was angry because I felt so helpless. I also noticed that some of the people who I thought were my closest friends became distant. I didn't realize that my cancer diagnosis was as hard on them as it was on me. When you're the one experiencing a cancer diagnosis, it's important to realize that cancer affects everyone. It's a family thing. They probably couldn't find the right words or maybe they were as terrified as I. Chances are my situation was forcing them to face their own vulnerability and mortality. I wanted to tell them, "I'm not dead. I'm just sick."

This is when you need your friends to be there for you, which makes a big difference when your world is so fragile. One of my friends gave me a little teddy bear to hold when I was afraid. Doing so helped me in knowing that someone cared and that they were thinking of me during that dark time when I felt so alone. Sometimes no words are adequate, but those thoughtful gestures keep you going when you don't know how you can face another day.

The anger was replaced by a deep sadness and then by fear again. The hardest part in coming to grips with the entire lengthy process of dealing with the surgery, low iodine diet, radiation treatment and getting adjusted to the correct dose of medicine, is knowing that you have this dreaded disease, but life keeps going on even though your own world has come crashing down. There are still all of the tasks of everyday life that don't go away: bills to pay, clothes to wash, meals to cook and kids to raise. It's hard to keep going when your life is so uncertain. I wondered, *how can the sun keep coming up each day when my world has become so dark?*

My mind flooded with the memories of when my dad, who I dearly loved, was dying from lung cancer. We had so many good visits when I took him to his chemo treatments. I'll never forget how he loved going to McDonald's afterwards for his beloved cheeseburger with extra cheese and his strawberry milkshake. I would have done anything to spare his life, but there was nothing anyone could do. He slowly began slipping away from us, beginning with his extreme fatigue and nausea from the chemo treatments, that little hat they gave him to wear, if he started losing his hair, and ultimately, the pain medication, hospice, and then . . . he was gone. Those last days I spent with him were so precious and too brief. When you love someone, you're never ready to say good-bye. No amount of time is ever enough.

I cried out, "Please, God. Spare my life. I want to see my son graduate from high school, and spend more time with my family. I want to really enjoy my grandchildren. I want to serve you by helping others. There's so much more I want to do. I still want to write that book."

Scripture:

I cried out of my distress to the Lord, and he heard me;

Jonah 2:2

Chapter Seven

The Surgery

I was told on Monday, August 27, that I had cancer, and on Friday of that week, August 31, I met with the surgeon. In the back of my mind, I was hoping that he would tell me that it was all a big mistake. Instead, he confirmed the diagnosis, which is what I knew in my heart was true.

One month later, I was scheduled to have a total thyroidectomy. Prior to surgery, I had to have all of the necessary pre-op tests, which consisted of a series of blood tests, a chest x-ray, a medical history, a full physical and an EKG. This was just the beginning.

My biggest concern was that the cancer hadn't spread to other parts of my body. My surgeon explained that they had no way of knowing that until after the surgery and total body scan.

I was so fortunate to have one of the best surgeons in the state. He was highly recommended by everyone I talked to. My other doctors informed me that he was the one they would have chosen had they been in my shoes. I cannot emphasize how important that was for me to hear.

Rain poured on the day of surgery, which matched my mood perfectly. I was in surgery for about seven hours. When I awoke in the recovery room, I was groggy and very short of breath, which the nurse explained was from the anesthesia. I was finally taken to my hospital room that evening. My family was all there, but I was too out of it to hardly notice. I was on oxygen all night and most of the next day. I was also nauseous the next day. Every time I lifted my head, I almost vomited. My voice was hoarse, and I was extremely weak.

I was sent home the next evening, overwhelmed with fatigue. It seemed so soon after such major surgery. Dazed and worn out, I wondered if I'd ever be myself again. Just a couple of months before, I didn't even know where my thyroid was much less its importance to the entire body. But I quickly learned that the thyroid controls most of our bodily functions and keeps everything moving smoothly. It's amazing how much that small organ in our body does. It makes hormones, which control heart rate, blood pressure, body temperatures and weight. Our moods can also be affected by our thyroid, because we need the correct dosage of thyroid hormone in order to function properly. Too much thyroid hormone can cause nervousness, restlessness, anxiety and irritability. Too little thyroid hormone can cause fatigue and depression, constipation and an overall feeling of sluggishness. I compare the thyroid to the proper running order of an automobile. When the car runs out of gas or the carburetor isn't working, the car will stop running. That's similar to how the thyroid works, which is essential to live a normal life. Without it, a person must take medication for the rest of their life.

I had a follow-up appointment with the surgeon a week later to make sure the incision was healing properly and so that he could check the stitches. While I was there, he gave me the surgical pathology report. I had a total of eight nodules throughout my thyroid gland with one of them, a solid mass, measuring over two centimeters. I had multifocal thyroid carcinoma involving the right lobe of my thyroid gland. Distant metastasis could not be assessed or, in other words, if there was invasion of the cancer outside the margin of my thyroid gland, but it was likely. There was no way of knowing until I had a total body scan. The doctor also informed me that I had another problem with my thyroid, called Hashimotos Thyroiditis. Some of the symptoms of this thyroid disorder can be sensitivity to cold, weight gain, weak muscles, depression, easily tired, forgetfulness, dry skin and hair, puffiness in the face, constipation, menstrual cycles can be altered, and heart conditions can be present. I only noticed a few of these symptoms. One month later, my endocrinologist and radiologist started preparing me for the body scan.

The body scan prep takes about six weeks. For two weeks before the scan, I had to be on a low-iodine diet, which meant no iodized salt, seafood, dairy products, canned or processed foods, lunch meats, or store-bought breads. Everything had to be fresh or homemade by following special recipes on the low-iodine diet. It was very important to use only the proper ingredients and to follow the diet closely in order to get accurate results from the body scan and radiation treatment.

I could feel life draining out of me with each passing day. Each day I became paler, and my face and eyes got puffier. I gained weight since I no longer had a thyroid, and I wasn't yet on any medicine to make my body function properly. I had no appetite and had to force myself to eat. My vision became blurry, and I had trouble concentrating. I wasn't on any thyroid medicine, so that any leftover cancer cells in my body would show up on the body scan. Unless someone has been through this, they would never realize how debilitating this can be, physically and emotionally. I remember having a groggy feeling in my head and I couldn't think clearly at all. All of my reflexes were slowed down. I felt like a zombie walking around with no feeling left in my body. By the time of the body scan, I found it difficult to move my lips to speak clearly, to use my hands, or even just pick up my feet to walk. The smallest activity became a chore.

Scripture:

But even the very hairs of your head are all numbered.
Matthew 10:30

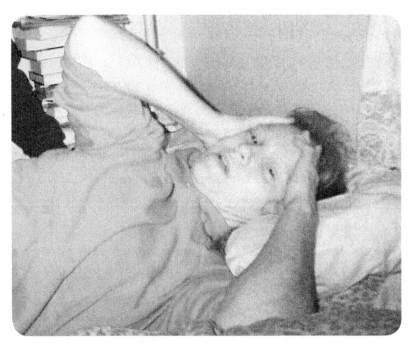

(This was me when I was too weak to get out of bed before the body scan and treatment. I was extremely hypothyroid, and getting weaker each day.)

Chapter Eight

The Radiation Treatment

I was scheduled for the total body scan and radiation treatment the week after Thanksgiving. Since I was on the low-iodine diet, I wasn't allowed to eat any of the traditional foods that are associated with Thanksgiving. But it didn't matter, because I didn't have an appetite. We didn't have our usual family get-together that year, as none of us felt like celebrating. It's a Thanksgiving that we will never forget.

During the week of the treatment, I had to go to the hospital each day to the nuclear medicine department for testing. Friday was the day of the treatment. When I arrived at the hospital on Monday morning, I was greeted by a friendly, jolly receptionist who made me feel right at home. I was anxious because I didn't know what to expect, but the staff tried to make me as comfortable as possible. By the end of the week, I knew them all by their first names.

The first part of the week was spent preparing me for the body scan and treatment. I had to swallow a capsule that contained small amounts of radioactive iodine (123), which was absorbed into my blood. Because thyroid tissue needs iodine to make thyroid hormone, the thyroid pulls the iodine out of the blood, which then accumulates in a person's thyroid cells. This Iodine is radioactive and sends out energy, which can be imaged with a special gamma camera to measure the radioactivity or uptake. After receiving the radioactive iodine, I returned to the hospital for the body scan. The results were then viewed by the radiologist, who determined that I did need a treatment. Radioactive Iodine (I-131) therapy is a treatment for thyroid cancer that kills cancer cells in the body after surgery, by using higher doses of radiation that the radiologist plans for the course of treatment.

When Friday morning arrived, I managed to find the strength to drive to the hospital once again. When I arrived in the nuclear medicine department, the staff took me in promptly for the treatment. I sat in a chair, and they placed sheets all around me and covered the floor as well. Wearing gloves, gowns, and masks so that they would not be exposed themselves, they carried in a steel container with a lid that contained the radiation, which was in capsule form.

I held my breath, thinking, "How can this be me? I hardly even take a Tylenol?" But I knew I had no other choice. I, reluctantly, popped the capsule into my mouth without touching it, knowing that little pill would keep me alive. I was kept at the hospital for two hours to make sure that I didn't get sick. I was instructed to go straight home so as not to expose anyone. I went to my car as quickly as possible. I just wanted to go home and get into bed, pull the covers up, and pretend this was all a bad dream. I was too tired and numb to care. With a body full of radiation, I had the uncanny feeling that I was auditioning for a part in the next James Bond movie.

As I drove home, I turned on the radio and listened to the news. In that moment, the world events didn't seem too important anymore, because I had my own little nuclear war going on inside my own body.

I got very nauseous that night and stayed that way for the next three days. By the third day, I couldn't eat, get out of bed, or even see well. Everything looked black; I felt like I was in a dark tunnel and was blending into it. My hands, feet, and lips were cold and lifeless. I felt much more dead than alive. From being off of my thyroid hormone so long, the doctor said that I was extremely hypothyroid, because of my abnormally low thyroid levels.

Scripture:

I know how to be abased and live humbly in straitened circumstances, and I know also how to enjoy plenty and live in abundance. I have learned in any and all circumstances the secret of facing every situation, whether well-fed or going hungry, having a sufficiency and enough to spare or going without or being in want. I have strength for all things in Christ who empowers me.

Philippians 4:12-13

Chapter Nine

Totally Isolated

That first weekend after the treatment was the hardest, as I had to be isolated from my family to ensure that they wouldn't be exposed to the radiation. They each stayed with different relatives for two weeks. This was my weakest moment, and yet I had to stay completely alone.

For about a week after the treatment, I noticed foods had a funny, almost-metallic taste. My mouth was also dry, so I had to drink a lot of fluids to stay hydrated and to help my kidneys remove the unused, radioactive iodine from my body. Eating sour candy like lemon drops helped. I started back on my thyroid medicine the following week and was allowed to eat a regular diet again. It took me a couple of weeks to get my appetite back. I started to regain my strength and appetite one day at a time.

Every woman knows, especially if she is a mother, how important it is to have some time just for yourself. No matter how much we love our families, everyone needs a little space once in awhile. It's a mother's deepest longing. Evenings can be especially hectic with small children not to mention downright insane with teenagers. From about 5:00 until about 9:00 p.m. is what I could almost painstakingly describe as the valley of the shadow of death. I won't even talk about evenings with teenagers. They have such chaotic schedules, and their music; we won't even go there. I can hear it now, even as I write, that pounding bass, in tune with every heartbeat. I'll save that for another book. It can drive a sane person crazy and wreck their nerves for a week. Do you remember that commercial, "Calgon, take me away"? The one where the mom is taking a relaxing bubble bath as she is trying to escape her world for a little while?

I admit that I've been guilty of yearning for that much-needed quiet time. I used to think, *"If I could just watch a good movie without any noise and actually see the end of it, or read a good book straight through, or sleep as long as I want to"*. I'm sure you understand what I mean.

But after being isolated for two weeks, I completely changed my mind. Like the saying, "Been there, done that," being alone was not nearly as glamorous as I thought it would be. There are only so many movies that I could watch, and only so many books that I could read. When I realized that, day after day, I was really alone, and no one would be walking through that door, it gave me plenty of time to contemplate that being alone was pretty lonely. Being alone began to take on a whole new meaning.

I probably got carried away, because I even made my family take our dog away. One day when I was feeling sorry for myself, I was elated to realize that my granddaughter's goldfish was still there. I remember saying to the fish, "Prince Charming, we're in this together." See, I told you I was lonely! I was so glad to see something else that was living and breathing. Sometimes, something as small as a goldfish can lift our spirits.

I was overly cautious about everything. I was afraid to even light a candle, and could just see the headlines in the newspaper, "Lady used as a bomb to test nuclear weapons following radiation treatment." You've got to admit, we hear some pretty bizarre things on the news these days.

Now that it's behind me, I have to almost chuckle at my naiveté, but at the time, it was a real concern. I had never been sick a day in my life, so it was a learning process for me.

Although I can usually find humor in almost any situation, this was one experience where I couldn't. That was a time in my life that I will never forget. It was not only difficult for me, but for my entire family as well. I did a lot of soul-searching, praying, and learning to yield my life to God's keeping. At that time, I didn't know the results of the treatment or even if it had been successful or not.

In the back of my mind, I went over and over all of the "what if's. What if the treatment didn't work? What if I need another one? What if all of my hair falls out? What if my family has to stay away longer? What if I'm too sick to take care of myself? And the final "what if"; What if I die? Those thoughts were never-ending.

Two weeks before Christmas, when most people were out shopping, I was home alone, too sick to do anything about it. I cried a lot as I listened to some of my favorite Christmas songs like "Have Yourself a Merry Little Christmas" and "The Christmas Shoes," because they only magnified my loneliness. I didn't realize before how many Christmas songs were about being home with your loved ones.

My mom was like a Christmas angel, filling in wherever she was needed. Brent took Travis to school on many snowy mornings. Mark kept working hard on his printing job, and his family helped as much as they could. My kids all tried cheering me up every chance they got.

We waved and blew kisses at one another from my front windows as they drove up and sat in front of our house for a little while, just to feel like they were home. They dropped off cards, pictures, and flowers. One card I'll always remember played the song, "I Will Survive." They even brought my favorite Starbucks drink, Strawberry Iced Frappacino. Savannah, my little granddaughter, was four years old at the time, and couldn't understand why I was all alone and why they couldn't come in. She thought everyone was mad at me. That took some careful explaining.

The ladies from church brought one meal after another, and I received many calls from neighbors and countless gifts and cards from friends. I realized how God had carried me through the storm when it was next to impossible to go on by myself. The famous poem "Footprints" came alive for me with a deeper meaning, as I realized that God had carried me at this terribly low time in my life. The last few lines of the poem had the most meaning, "The times when you have seen only one set of footprints is when I carried you."

I was now beginning to understand the depth of God's love.

Keep and guard me as the pupil of your eye; hide me in the shadow of your wings.

Psalm 17:8

Thus says the Lord: Restrain your voice from weeping and your eyes from tears, for your work shall be rewarded, says the Lord; and your children shall return from the enemy's land. And there is hope for your future, says the Lord.

Jeremiah 31:16-17

Chapter Ten

I'll Be Home for Christmas

My time of total isolation was finally nearing an end.

Two weeks later, as I drove to the hospital on the morning of my final body scan, where I learned that the treatment had been successful and the cancer was gone, I lifted a little prayer toward heaven, which was enough to dispel all of the anxious thoughts that were going through my mind.

When I called home to break the good news to my family, there was dead silence on both ends of the phone. There were no words to express the thankfulness we had in our hearts at that moment. I had waited for so long to hear those two words, "cancer free"!

When I returned home from the hospital, I wrote a letter to my family and friends straight from my heart. I poured out all of the feelings that I'd been holding inside for so long. The timing was just perfect, as it was two weeks before Christmas. What a gift!

To All of My Family and Friends:

There is such a tender and special place in my heart for all of you. I will always remember the amazing love that you have given me at this difficult time in all of our lives. I will cherish it forever.

Mark, I've seen you wipe away many a tear in your own quiet way, but you had to keep on going anyway through it all. You were so strong for me when I was so weak. You were my hero. Thank you for being there for me.

Mom, you have never given up believing that I would get better. I know there were many times that you wanted to scream without my hearing you. Thank you for always being there for me to talk to. You helped me get through so many days. I honestly can't imagine a single day without you.

Sarah, you have been going through so much in your own life like a recent marriage and a baby on the way. Even while raising a family of your own, you have always been there for me. You were so much help, even when your heart was breaking.

Bethany, you have helped everywhere you've been needed, and you never asked for anything in return. You have given your love and time so unselfishly. I'll always remember hearing you say, "I love you, Mommy," as you kissed me softly on the cheek. Your gentle love crossed barriers where mere words just weren't enough.

Travis, my precious teenage son, I know it's been a hard year for you. I'm sure it was difficult to feel normal at such a busy time in high school. When other kids your age are in the process of growing up, you had to keep on marching in the band, even when you didn't feel like it. But instead, you had to fight back the tears, wondering what all of our futures would hold. Maybe someday, you will understand the depth of my love for you and how proud that I am of you.

Savannah and Landon, my little grandbaby angels, I love you for simply being who you are. You've inspired me and made me laugh at times when nothing else was funny. You've shown me how to see life through your tender eyes, something that only a child can do. You gave me much-needed hope.

Savannah, I love your laughter and singing and those little girly giggles. Landon, we have so much catching up to do. Even though I was there when you were born and heard you cry for the very first time, I haven't felt like myself for quite awhile. At that moment of your birth, when life was so new to you and so unsure for me, I realized how precious life truly is. It can quickly pass us by. I will never take another day for granted again.

The time for rejoicing is here. The time for singing has come. God has wiped away all of our tears. Let us rejoice together. It's time to come home now. I love all of you so much! We can sing "I'll Be Home for Christmas" together. We have what is truly the most important. We have love, hugs, and one another. And we have good food to eat. There are cookies to bake, and don't forget the fudge. We have our health, even if it's just for today!

Most of all, we have the most precious gift of all, which is God's Son. We have the assurance of eternal life!

Scripture:

The Lord your God is in the midst of you, a Mighty One, a Savior who saves! He will rejoice over you with joy; He will rest and in His love he will be silent and make no mention of past sins, or even recall them; He will exult over you with singing.
Zephaniah 3:17

Chapter Eleven

The Following Year

As the New Year settled in, I was still very tired and yet hopeful of the future. I was so glad to be back on my thyroid medicine and normal diet. What a difference that little pill makes! It's so easy to take the slightest things for granted because we don't realize what a major role they play in our daily lives.

I couldn't wait to get back to normal and to pick up where I left off before my cancer diagnosis, but I got discouraged because, as hard as I tried, I just didn't feel like my old self. The word "normal" took on a whole new meaning, as feeling good for several days, and then being overwhelmed by fatigue without warning was my "new normal." Only a short time ago, I felt like taking on the world. I had always known the meaning of the word, *Vitality!*

I rested a lot during that entire winter, sleeping in and taking it easy as much as possible. That time of rest helped me get my energy back. I eased back into my routine; I was so fortunate that I didn't have to work much at that stage of the healing process. I realize many people don't have that choice, which makes healing that much harder. I didn't think it would be so difficult to regain my energy, but my doctor told me that it takes awhile for the body to bounce back after having surgery. I had one cold after another that winter because my immunity was so low.

I went to my endocrinologist every three months for the first year to have my blood checked, to make sure my medicine was the correct dosage. The medicine had to be adjusted and readjusted at different intervals to get it stabilized. Also, they monitored, very closely, my blood work to make sure the cancer was not returning. My doctor told me that the longer you go without a recurrence, the better the prognosis. They like to keep the medicine elevated to help prevent a recurrence. My blood was also checked periodically for rising thyroglobulin levels which could mean that the cancer may have returned.

During the spring as the weather started getting better, my energy started improving. There's something about that good, old sunshine that seems to be a natural healer, because it always lifts my spirits. I was able to get outside and move around more. I walked my dog, Maggie, daily and played Frisbee and soccer outside in the yard with her. I also played outside with Savannah and Landon. We all really loved the fresh air and the sunshine, which was good for all of us. I spent as much time as I could doing yard work and planting flowers. There's something about getting your hands dirty and enjoying nature that seems to usher you directly into the presence of God. It's good therapy for the soul.

When I felt good and had energy, I kept busy, but when I noticed that I was feeling more tired than usual, I rested. I had to learn to pace myself and not overdo it. That was an art in itself, because I had never done that in my entire life. For as long as I could remember, I always had a surplus of energy. My doctor told me not to get discouraged and reminded me that I wasn't twenty years old anymore. She was right, but I was the last one to admit it.

By the fall, I was feeling great again. Finally! It was one year after my cancer diagnosis, but what a year it had been. It was one of those things that you go through because you have to, but when you look back, you wonder how you ever did it. I was starting to get my energy back without tiring so easily, and it felt good to get back to life! I remember many days when I was too weak to get out of bed. I wanted to get up and tackle the world, but I just didn't have the stamina. I would lie in bed, staring at the ceiling and wonder how I would ever feel the same again. Somewhere, deep down inside I believed that it was only a trial I had to go through, and when I got through it, I would be so much better, because my entire perspective on life had been changed.

I went back to the endocrinologist for a checkup and to have my blood checked every three months after the surgery and radiation. One year after the radiation, in December, my doctor informed me that I needed more follow up tests to recheck for a recurrence. It was routine, but I was unaware that I had to go through the entire total body scan protocol. I was just starting to feel good again, but I understood that I now needed lifelong monitoring to be on the safe side.

In February, seventeen months after my surgery, and fifteen months after the radiation, I started the entire process all over again. To monitor thyroid cancer closely and to take all of the necessary precautions, it is lengthy, but necessary. I had to go off my thyroid medication, and at the end of March, I started the low-iodine diet. My body was completely depleted of all energy once again, and I became extremely hypothyroid. Unfortunately,

I knew that feeling all too well, but it seemed much harder now because I was working. We had a small family cleaning business. I didn't work too much, but I didn't have the necessary energy that I needed to get through my own day, without doing anything else. It was so difficult to keep going every day when all I felt like doing was staying in bed and pulling the covers over my head. Becoming hypothyroid has an enormous effect on your emotions, not to mention the physical effects which are similar to a full-blown case of PMS, only worse, and that last much longer than usual. I was so tired and emotional, and my body felt so puffy and bloated that I wondered when I would explode. To make matters worse, when they did the blood work, the pregnancy test they took as a precaution came back on the borderline, so I had to have the blood work repeated. I knew without any doubt that I wasn't pregnant, and, of course, I was right. I was sure that one day I would be able to look back and laugh at the uncertain pregnancy test. I felt so bad that my body was tricked into thinking that I was *pregnant*. Our hormones can really rule!

For some reason, the low-iodine diet was harder than the first time. I ate a lot of fruits and vegetables and made some different recipes, but I got so bored with it and finally didn't feel like cooking at all. I was starving for foods that I wasn't allowed to have. I was learning what a "Big Mac Attack" was all about. One day when I was at the grocery store, all I could do was cry. Eventually, the longer I was off my medicine, nothing tasted good to me at all. I completely lost my appetite all the while gaining weight. It just didn't seem fair.

I was beginning to feel like Dr. Jekyll and Mr. Hyde, and wished everyone would quit experimenting with my body like I was a guinea pig and leave me alone. By that point, it seemed to me that they had done just about everything but embalm me.

The hardest part the second time around was the fact that I felt so awful and no one else really understood. No matter how hard I tried to explain what I was going through, they couldn't relate because they had never been in my position. There were times when I felt so alone and frightened and wasn't sure how I could go on one more day.

I had to go to the hospital every day for a week, like before, for the radioactive iodine 123 uptake to be prepared for the body scan. The nuclear medicine technologist told me it wasn't unlikely for people to have a recurrence. They were planning another radiation treatment on Friday unless the whole body scan came out clean. It just so happened that this particular Friday was Good Friday.

Scripture:

For I know the thoughts and plans that I have for you, says the Lord, thoughts and plans for welfare and peace and not for evil, to give you hope in your final outcome.

Jeremiah 29:11

Part Three

There Can Be Life after a Cancer Diagnosis

We're finally to my favorite part of the book, which is the focal point. I'm so excited to share with you everything I have learned from my personal experience with thyroid cancer.

The first two sections of this book have been all about me, but I'm about to turn things around and put the major emphasis on you. I want to offer you hope and to encourage you to hold your head up high and take hold of the reality that a cancer diagnosis doesn't always have to mean the end.

As you read this part of the book, you will learn to become active. It's about your doing some things that will make a positive difference in your life. It's about you taking a proactive approach to face this disease head on and fight it with all your might.

As you learn to work through some of the problems that you are facing, my earnest prayer is that you will become hopeful and learn what true rejoicing is all about. Those bitter tears can be replaced by shouts of joy! It can happen to you!

Chapter Twelve

The Nearness of God

I felt so alone during the days leading up to the body scan. Every day I prayed for God to give me the strength to just get through this experience. For the first time, I learned what it meant to pray without ceasing. I ran to God, and he filled my soul with his presence. There is just no other way to describe it other than the nearness of God.

I knew that I wasn't alone anymore. He was there in his gentle, loving way, prodding me to keep going on day after day. So many Scriptures came alive to me. I would awaken in the middle of the night, and I would think of another scripture. I can only say that by the grace of God, he was strengthening me, because I couldn't focus or think clearly about anything else. Everything became cloudy to me, except for the presence of God. It was as if he walked through the fire with me. Whether I was in the shower, driving my car, or doing something else, Scripture after Scripture flooded my mind. They were all positive and uplifting. I knew that God was comforting me and leading my every step. The weaker

I felt, the stronger I felt the presence of God. It reminded me of the scripture. 2 Corinthians 12: 10, So for the sake of Christ, I am well pleased and take pleasure in infirmities, insults, hardships, persecutions, perplexities, and distresses; for when I am weak, then am I strong. The one scripture that helped me the most was Psalm 126:5-6, They who sow in tears shall reap in joy and singing. He who goes forth bearing seed and weeping shall doubtless come again with rejoicing bringing his sheaves with him. Day by day, I couldn't get that one scripture out of my mind. It was as if God was telling me that this present suffering that I was going through was only temporary. I might be crying now, but soon I will be full of joy once again and be singing. He has done just that. That one scripture is the foundation for this book, *Rejoicing through the Tears*. I believe with all of my heart that he wants you to believe it too! `

I was so thankful that God had deepened my faith and given me joy at that time, because lying under a body scan is frightening, and you realize that it will reveal your destiny. As I lay with my arms at my sides, I closed my eyes and didn't look up. Mere words could not express what I felt at that moment. To this day, I can't explain it, but it still brings tears to my eyes. I have never felt such peace. I'm not sure what happened in that body scan, but whatever it was, my life has been changed forever, and I will never be the same. It was glorious! I have never felt such love in my entire life. A Dazzling, bright light flashed through my mind's eye. Although my eyes were closed, the brightness consumed my spirit. It was nothing you could see with your eyes, but it was so much deeper than that. It was as if God reached down and touched me. It was just him and me. Nothing else mattered. It was as if he put his stamp of approval on me and was giving me the power and the strength to move forward. I was surrounded by his glory and he has never left my side since. Now, everything I do and everywhere I go, he is right there with me, leading me in the brightness of his presence. There was a vast, overpowering love that only could have come from God, because he is love. All of those times as a child in Sunday school were so much more meaningful now. I was not only singing those hymns with my lips, but now with my heart. He became my best friend and the stronghold of my life. He has become my strength and my song, because of his great love for me.

At that moment, I realized how precious I was in God's sight. My life was so special to him that he was rejoicing over me with singing. How awesome! I have never known such intense love.

My life was all up to him. He held the keys to my future. If the report was a good one or if he decided to take me to heaven, I was finally at peace with his master plan. He was abiding within me. He was there to stay, and he wasn't going anywhere.

He will do this for anyone who calls upon him, not just for me. He is closer than your next breath and only a heartbeat away. Life is so fragile. Cancer puts all your priorities in order.

We all know the economy isn't good. If we look around us and watch the news for just a couple of minutes, we realize this world is in turmoil. Even though we are a part of what is going on all around us, we need to realize that God is still in control and nothing can take place without his permission. Nothing can ever separate us from his love.

Times are bleak and we may have to endure some rough times for a moment, but we can take comfort in knowing he will go through it with us, and still bring us out better than when we first went in. He is a mighty fortress that we can run to in any storm that we have to face. We can learn how to praise him even during the most difficult days.

As we look at the light shining in the distance, the more we focus on it and the closer it gets to us, it becomes brighter. It permeates our very soul with God's own presence. God is so real. When we've lost all hope, he becomes our only hope. When we're weak, he is our only strength. When we're frightened, he becomes our only peace. Since God has spared my life, I want to please him and serve him in any way that he requires. He has a plan for each person's life. He wants you to live with passion, meaning, and enthusiasm. Now, I want to live each moment as if it were the last.

About an hour after the body scan, the radiologist called me into his office, where my results were hanging up on the x-ray screen. He told me, "This is a very good report. Everything looks wonderful. There is no sign of a recurrence or metastasis anywhere in your body. This is a perfectly clean scan. This is good news!"

I asked him when I could resume my thyroid medicine and regular diet. "It's 11:31 now," he said. "How about 11:32? And by the way, have a great Easter!" I was elated. The first thing I did on the way home was grab a Big Mac!

Looking back to that Christmas when I was in isolation, I compare it to Jesus, coming as a little baby to give hope to the world. And when I was given such good news on Easter, Jesus's resurrection from death took on more meaning than I had ever thought possible. Never give up hope!

Scripture:

But those who wait for the Lord shall change and renew their strength and power; they shall lift their wings and mount up as eagles; they shall run and not be weary, they shall walk and not faint or become tired.

Isaiah 40:31

I will lift up my eyes to the hills. From whence shall my help come? My help comes from the Lord, Who made heaven and earth.

Psalm 121:1-2

For I know that my Redeemer and Vindicator lives, and at last He will stand upon the earth. And after my skin, even this body, has been destroyed, then from my flesh or without it I shall see God, Whom I, even I, shall see for myself and on my side! And my eyes shall behold Him, and not as a stranger! My heart pines away and is consumed within me.

Job 19:25-27

Arise (from the depression and prostration in which circumstances have kept you-rise to a new life!) Shine (be radiant with the glory of the Lord), for your light has come, and the glory of the Lord has risen upon you! For behold, darkness shall cover the earth, and dense darkness, all peoples, but the Lord shall rise upon you, and his glory shall be seen on you.

Isaiah 60:1-2

Chapter Thirteen

The Midnight Hour

As this book progresses, I feel the need to address a topic that we all must face at some point in our lives. A time in our lives when we feel completely alone, without hope, and utterly forsaken. When our back is up against the wall, and we feel that there is no way out. This could come as a result of a cancer diagnosis or some other illness or possibly a financial crisis, a divorce, or problems with a child or a parent. No matter what the problem, there is one common characteristic: We feel completely alone. What then? What do we do when we find ourselves in the Midnight Hour?

My journey back has been a cumbersome one, a long, drawn-out trial. It was a very real Midnight Hour in my life. And there have been many hurdles along the way.

As I was reflecting on this topic, I realized that Jesus, being the son of God, felt the same loneliness that we all have to endure, only much more, because he took on the sins of the entire human race. Jesus had great emotion. He cried at the death of his beloved friend, Lazarus, before he brought him back to life. Although, he knew he had the power to resurrect Lazarus, he still wept because he cared so deeply for him.

While in the Garden of Gethsemane, he sweat great drops of blood, knowing what he was about to endure for you and for me. He felt extremely alone in his Midnight Hour as he asked his disciples if they could just stay awake with him for a little while longer, which they didn't do. He must have felt completely abandoned at that moment. Ultimately, as he was dying on the cross, he suffered like no one ever has. He felt completely alone in that Midnight Hour of his life as he called out to God, in Matthew 27:46 And about the ninth hour Jesus cried with a loud voice, My God, My God, why have you abandoned me? During that moment, he was completely alone. He had to experience total separation from God, as God had to turn his back on his son and walk away so that he could give us eternal life. Jesus didn't have to do it, but he did out of love, because he knew what it would mean to those he was dying for. Now, that's love.

No matter what we are going through, there is victory over any darkness in our lives. What we believe about our future determines how we live today. For example, when we're planning a vacation, we make all the necessary preparations. Likewise, we need to do the same to prepare for heaven, because it's every bit as real as the Bahamas, only more so. We spend so much time preparing for things that are here today and gone tomorrow and such little time planning where we will spend eternity. Our outlook each day greatly influences how we live our lives from day to day, but our faith and beliefs are what mold our future and all of eternity. As you can see in the following scripture, our faith makes all the difference. Mark, 5:34, He said to her, Daughter, your faith, has restored you to health. Go in peace and be continually healed and freed from your disease.

Some people think that God will do everything instantly in their lives. Sometimes he does, but more often he allows us to go through trials so that we will learn from our suffering

Even during our Midnight Hour, God is always faithful. His love is so constant that we can count on it. When we've had all that we can take, he lifts us up and carries us in his everlasting arms with the strength of the mighty eagle where we find shelter from the cares of the world around us.

Remember that today's delays during your Midnight Hour are often tomorrow's victories. Just like he is no stranger to loneliness, pain, and rejection, he is also no stranger to miracles that can happen when faith is present.

Jesus will calm the storms in our lives, and he has all authority over our Midnight Hour. Nothing can separate us from his love. Just like he told the paralytic, in John 5:8, to "Get up! Pick up your mat and walk"; he wants us to do something also. Our faith must be alive and growing from day to day for miracles to occur.

As we realize that we are surrounded by the glory of his presence and learn to touch the hem of his garment, our faith will be ignited, and he will come to us, walking on the water of our sorrow and tears. There will be a day when Jesus will comfort with all comfort. We will be able to sit on his lap like a little child, and he will hold us in his loving, fatherly arms and will wipe away all our tears.

I had many ups and downs during the Midnight Hour of my life. On my road to recovery after that amazing experience I had in the body scan, it hasn't always been easy, but God has always been there to help me in my human frailties and pick me back up again. That's what I love about God. He knows us better than anyone else ever will and he still loves us. He's a personal God. One night after the body scan I wasn't feeling well. I hadn't regained my energy as fast as I wanted to. I went to bed that night very discouraged. I had the most amazing dream. I really believe this is where I found joy, just as the scripture says, in Psalm 16:11, You will show me the path of life; in your presence is fullness of joy, at Your right hand there are pleasures forevermore. God knows how to get our attention. It went like this . . . .

I fell into bed utterly exhausted, and sweet sleep became my best friend, as I was pulled into dreams of pure peace. All at once, that same bright light that I experienced in the body scan was back. My world was luminous once again. I looked down, and all I could see was dazzling white and brightness all around me. I could see his white robe and sandals.

I looked up, and I could see Jesus walking, peacefully, into my Midnight Hour. He was all love and authority, and my soul was saturated with joy. As he entered my life, the sweet perfume of his presence touched everything that concerned me. Everything was amazingly brought to life and miraculously changed within a moment, as I realized that, for where he is, I am made whole. Everything is possible to him that believes.

He drew closer to me. I knelt down at his feet; streams of dazzling light shimmered through his nail-scarred hands and feet. "Jesus!" I cried, And he answered, "I Am!" He bid me to stay and linger in the glory of his presence. He hastened to tell me, "You're never alone, my child; Never alone. If only you could fathom the depth of my love for you and the great things that I have prepared for you!"

His beautiful yet piercing eyes met mine and they could see right into my soul. He knew me completely, and everything that concerned me, concerned him. He could speak to my spirit without saying a word. He knew my every thought before I could think it.

He tilted his head back and released a joyful, hearty laugh, and then I knew everything would be alright. We sat down together in my Midnight Hour and had a picnic, as the angels rejoiced over us, because all calm and light were restored. All was well, at last. I awoke with a new perspective on life.

Soon after that glorious dream, I felt the prompting of God. It was a stirring in my spirit, like never before. I've never felt so strong about anything in my life. I sensed God telling me to write this book to offer hope to anyone who is going through their Midnight Hour. I've had this driving force ever since. I will not rest until I get these words out.

There is hope for you in your Midnight Hour, my friend. Never give up!

Scripture:

For His anger is but for a moment, but His favor is for a lifetime or in His favor is life. Weeping may endure for a night, but joy comes in the morning.

Psalm 30:5

To Everything there is a season, and a time for every matter or purpose under heaven: A time to be born and a time to die, a time to plant and a time to pluck up what is planted. A time to weep and a time to laugh, a time to mourn and a time to dance.

Ecclesiastes 3:1-2, 4

You have turned my mourning into dancing for me; You have put off my sackcloth and girded me with gladness. To the end that my tongue and my heart and everything glorious within me may sing praise to You and not be silent. O Lord my God, I will give thanks to you forever.

Psalm 30: 11-12

For He will turn your mourning into dancing!

And he did!

<u>From Bitter Tears to Heartfelt Rejoicing</u>

<u>He Has Brought Me Out of the Miry Clay</u>

<u>And Put My Feet On Solid Ground</u>

<u>My Darkness Has Been Turned To Light</u>

<u>Out Of the Ashes I Rise</u>

<u>With A New Song and Dance</u>

<u>For I Now Know What It Means</u>

<u>To</u>

<u>Rejoice Through My Tears!</u>

Rejoicing through My Tears

I sit alone, quietly, in the twilight
Pondering over the long dreary day
My head hung low, with a forlorn sigh
So alone in the dark, with a tear in my eye

As evening gives way to the dark all around
I am startled by a different sound.
I reluctantly gaze up into the sky
And I am suddenly aware that it's just my Maker and I.

In the distance, I can see him walking up that hill
At the foot of the cross, I kneel
He tells me he has a plan for me to fulfill
But first, I must be still

As I am traveling through this dry and weary land
I can hear footsteps in the sand
All it took was just one touch from his nail scarred hand
To give me the strength to stand

Through the long watches of the night
Through the dark and the gray
He hears me when I cry
He hears me when I pray

Brenda George

Even when the lightning flashes and the thunder rolls
I can feel him near
He died for all lost souls
He cares about each and every tear

All at once the storm calms and night gives way to day
When all my cares at the foot of the cross I lay
I look up and behold a rainbow
And it is then that I know

I'm not the only one traveling this sod
There's someone who really loves me
And this same path has trod
He daily leads me with his staff and his rod

It's my Father, My God
The Lord of my life
He whispers my name
And he renews my life!

His eyes meet mine and after awhile
I am caught up in his warm smile
He tells me to be glad
Not dejected and sad

I have a new song to sing with my savior and King
He has done a great and mighty thing
My heart sings and my heart cries
On the wings of the morning, my spirits rise

With my head held high
In just one glance
He lifts me up
And we start to dance

I have never been so happy
To hear his voice
There is none anywhere like him
All of heaven will rejoice.

Chapter Fourteen

Things I've Learned The Hard Way

I am so anxious to share all these things that God has laid on my heart for you, which is why this book has been written. First, I will list the different topics that I will be sharing with you, and then I will break them down into more manageable concepts. Some of these topics might not be a major concern when you have first been diagnosed, but you might benefit from some of the knowledge I've learned as you are recovering.

The topics I will address are:

1. Allow your feelings to come out.
2. Avoid self-pity at all costs.
3. Trust God completely no matter what.
4. Take one day at a time.
5. Live with zeal and enthusiasm.
6. Never take one single day for granted, and have a thankful heart.
7. Don't get mad over small things.

8. Learn to see life through the eyes of a child.
9. Watch how you treat others.
10. Learn to laugh a lot!
11. Balance is key. Learn to say "no."
12. Do things you enjoy.
13. Surround yourself with happy, positive people.
14. Get organized.
15. Tune out the bad things.
16. Don't procrastinate.
17. Develop a healthy self-esteem.
18. Never give up. Fight the good fight.
19. Don't compare yourself to others.
20. Learn to forgive.
21. Enjoy nature.
22. Make each day a celebration.
23. You can get fit and healthy again.

1. **Allow your feelings to come out.**

    This is very important. There are many stages you will go through after hearing those dreadful words, and all of the feelings are normal. Getting to where the news actually sinks in is a step-by-step process. Don't try to keep these feelings bottled up or eventually they will become like poison inside of you. Find a friend or family member to talk to or join a cancer support group. There's help available to anyone who needs it.

    Remember that you are not alone, although there will be times when you will feel like you are. But there are others who feel the same way you do. If you look around, you will always find someone with a worse scenario than yours. Upon seeing their situation, you will be thankful for your own problems.

Let your feelings come out. If you feel like crying, then cry. If you feel like screaming, by all means scream. Eventually, you will have to just let go and be who you are. Before long, you may even feel like laughing again. I know I did. It just takes time. We want everything instant these days, but our emotions don't work that way. We can't just flip a switch on or off to react a certain way. God never intended for people to be that way. We are so much more complex than that. You can't hurry through your emotions. The recuperation and healing process takes time, emotionally and physically. Although you may not realize it, this is when your learning and growth begins.

2. **Avoid self-pity at all costs.**

    When I was first diagnosed with cancer, I went through a myriad of emotions, self-pity being one of them. One of the first questions you will probably ask is why is this happening to me? It's perfectly normal to feel that way at first. We usually start by blaming God, someone else, or even ourselves. You might think, *If only I'd taken better care of myself, eaten healthier, exercised more, or hadn't been so stressed.* Yes, all of those factors contribute to our overall health, but we shouldn't blame anyone, including ourselves.

    We have to look at the big picture. If we live long enough, we are bound to go through some bumps along the way. It's called life. The sooner we learn to face our difficulties, the sooner the healing process will begin. Cancer is no respecter of persons. It hits people of every age, race, rich, poor, and, yes, even people that appear to be the picture of health. It even hits athletes. There is no logical explanation; cancer has stumped millions of excellent physicians for decades. Mentally wrestling with why does no good. The sooner we learn to face our plight, the sooner we learn to fight it.

When I was first diagnosed, I withdrew from the world for awhile. I was in shock and needed time to grasp my situation. As hard as it was for me then, I have to admit now that I've grown so much. Now I want to reach out to others more than ever.

As much as I'd like to ease the pain that others are going through, it's something that each person must work through on their own. I'm not talking about support from others, which I will discuss later. What I'm saying is, you are the one who must learn how to deal with your cancer diagnosis and come to grips with how to handle it. When we allow self-pity to linger too long, we become bitter and resentful of others and of life in general, which will delay the healing process. We must learn to release all of those feelings. When we do, we gradually start improving in all aspects of our lives.

3. **Trust God completely no matter what.**

And I mean *completely*. It may not be easy at first, especially if everything has been roses up until now. Unfortunately for many of us, it takes a crisis to bring us to our knees. It is that humble, childlike faith and trust that moves the mighty hand of God. That helpless moment is when we realize our own feeble weakness and that we lack the power to control what is taking place, which can be very frightening. There is no other way out, but to surrender everything to God. This is easier said than done, but in the whole scheme of things, what other choice is there? God specializes in fixing our problems and cleaning up our messes. And that includes cancer. He's in the miracle-working business and has all the credentials. It's just a matter of how much faith you have in him. He is waiting on you to come to him for help and to believe in your heart that he desires to help you. Once you fully grasp how much he loves you and take hold of the truth that he can do so much more than you can even ask of him, that's when peace comes in. But you have to be willing to let go and put your full trust in him.

I know not everyone gets better. People die every day. This is where we have to trust that God has a different plan. He knows what he is doing. He doesn't love those people any less. One thing I learned from my experience is that when I get to my weakest moment, that's when God is there, right on time. When everything is going well, and I'm doing just fine all by myself, I rely on myself more. It's easier to push God away when life is going well.

One of the key factors that have helped me is to stand on the word of God and to apply the Scriptures to my daily living, which is why I have put Scripture passages throughout this book. I want them to sink into your heart and saturate your spirit with the awesome promises of God.

Although this has been a long journey, I am learning to rest in God and trust that I'm in his safekeeping. Life can be uncertain at times. You may be fighting cancer or something else that feels insurmountable to you. You may be doing everything humanly possible to get well, and you should, but ultimately, he's the one who has your life in his hands. Don't ever let anyone tell you that there is no hope. I know that things can look pretty desperate, but as long as there is faith, there is hope. You just have to learn to let go of doubt and at the same time, grab hold of hope and never let it go. God makes no mistakes. He has a plan for your life, but how you live out that plan is entirely up to you.

At some point in time, we will all have to endure some type of a trial. You can count on it. That's just life. How we are before or after our trial is not what's important, but rather, how we respond to adversity while we are going *through* it! Notice that I said *through*. We don't stay in our trial. We pass through it. You can talk to God straight from your heart. It doesn't have to be all churchy. Just be yourself. There is a Scripture that really speaks to my heart, Psalm 46:10, "Be still and know that I am God." Although very simple, this passage contains a wealth of wisdom. We just need to learn to be quiet and enter into God's resting place. Once we are quiet in his presence, he can do his work in and through us. He's our shepherd, friend, and eternal rock.

Something that I find amazing is how roses can bloom in the middle of the desert. If we are still long enough to notice these small miracles that are right in front of us, they can often teach us a valuable lesson about life. Those roses can be compared to us. Once we take hold of the love that God speaks into our lives, we, too, can open up and bloom in the most unlikely places. We can bloom like we never believed possible, even if it's in a dry and weary land.

There may be things in your life that you can't control, like it or not. Those are the things you need to turn over to him and leave at the foot of the cross. When you can finally learn to do that, you will be free from worry, so that you can live the best you can be for today and all the days to come.

You are in the middle of a storm right now, but soon you will be *through* it, and eventually the rainbow will appear. All you have to do is reach up for it, and God will embrace your hand. At that moment, you will know that he is smiling down on you.

Scripture:

Lean on, trust in, and be confident in the Lord with all your heart and mind and do not rely on your own insight or understanding. In all your ways know, recognize, and acknowledge Him and He will direct and make straight and plain your paths.

Proverbs 3:5-6

Now to Him Who, by the power that is at work within us, is able to do super-abundantly, far over and above all that we ask or think. (Infinitely beyond our highest prayers, desires, thoughts, hopes or dreams) is able to do immeasurably more than all we ask or imagine, according to his power that is at work within us.

Ephesians 3:20

Behold, I am doing a new thing! Now it springs forth; do you not perceive and know it and will you not give heed to it? I will even make a way in the wilderness and rivers in the desert.

Isaiah 43:19

4. **Take one day at a time.**

    While reading my Bible recently, I came upon something that really spoke to me. In Exodus, God sent Moses to deliver the Israelites from their hard lives in Egypt. They were being oppressed with many burdens and were in great bondage. They were being held against their will by Pharaoh, the king of Egypt. He made their lives bitter by hard work and he dealt harshly with them. But God had a different plan. He heard their cries. He wanted to deliver them from the hand of the Egyptians into a larger land; a land of plenty flowing with milk and honey. It was their Promised Land by God. It all sounds great, but it wasn't easy. They had many trials to go through along the way. After they finally got permission from Pharaoh to leave Egypt, God led them through the wilderness. The path he took them on was rugged. It wasn't easy. I really believe he took them that way to teach them a valuable lesson. He wanted them to learn to lean on him when the going got rough. God led them by day in a pillar of a cloud and a pillar of fire by night. Pharaoh and the Egyptians changed their minds and decided to come after them and not let them go. God parted the Red Sea and led the Israelites right through the middle, but all of the Egyptians were killed. What a powerful loving God! He can part our sea of trouble and lead us straight on through to our Promised Land.

When the Israelites first left Egypt, they were excited about the possibilities that awaited them, and they praised and worshipped God for delivering them. They were on the way to the Promised Land, but in order to get there, they had to go *through* the wilderness first. They were in a Midnight Hour of their own. They were hungry. Once again, God heard their cries and he sent down manna, or bread, from heaven to sustain them. The long journey they were starting wasn't easy, but God sent enough manna for each person each day. After awhile, they grew weary, much like you and I do, when we're on the way to our Promised Land of good health, or whatever we are striving for. They started grumbling and complaining. God noticed their unthankful attitudes and mistrust in him, even after all he had done for them, and the many miracles that he performed while bringing them from their captivity. Their murmuring and complaining prolonged their journey even more. This is so true of the many things we face in our day-to-day lives and reminds me of how I felt when I was on the low-iodine diet. I thought that journey would never end. But it taught me to be thankful for each new day, whatever God sends my way, knowing that he is with me on each and every journey. I had to learn to depend on God for each day's renewed strength. Once I could get to that place of trusting him, even in the wilderness, I realized that my spirit was refreshed and he gave me just enough strength to face the next day and to let me know that I am never alone.

God wants us to put our full trust in him and to live one day at a time, even with all of our unanswered questions. I have realized that once you fight one battle, there are usually many more to fight. I believe that God wants us to hand each day's battles over to him. He knows our strengths and our weaknesses and wants us to learn to depend on him for our every need. Because of his incredible love for us, he desires to bless us abundantly, but he also wants us to learn to lean heavily on him, casting all of our worries and cares upon him, because he is able.

God allows us to go through some things that seem hard at the moment in order to learn a valuable lesson. In the end, we can usually say we are the better for it. It doesn't happen overnight. Hopefully, it won't take forty years. It is a process. I have learned from this passage in the bible and my experience, to trust God one day at a time and to have a good attitude. He can meet me right where I am and give me strength for the next day. Everything is easier, little by little. There will always be many things that we will have to tackle along this journey called Life. Some of them could be: saving money, losing weight, recuperating from an illness, coping with the loss of a loved one, going through a nasty divorce, raising an unruly teenager, or even tackling an insurmountable project. Your goals may be more attainable by taking baby steps. They can be achieved much more easily by breaking them down into smaller more manageable concepts. Each day's problems are enough to worry about. Some days you may wonder if you will just be able to hold on until tomorrow. We can't afford to get all flustered; worrying about tomorrow before it even gets here. I try not to think too far down the road, but I do have both short—and long-range goals. I make a to-do list each day and have learned to cross off things that I accomplish and to leave until tomorrow those things I didn't get done, knowing that tomorrow is another day. We must learn to live each day to the fullest without worrying about the next day. No one, including those who have never had cancer, knows what tomorrow may bring. No one has a single guarantee for even one more day or of one more breath, for that matter. So breathe in deeply while taking in all the goodness that each day can offer.

Scripture:

The Lord spread a cloud for a covering (by day), and a fire to give light in the night. The Israelites asked, and He brought quails and satisfied them with the bread of heaven. He opened

the rock, and water gushed out; it ran in the dry places like a river. For He earnestly remembered his holy word and promise to Abraham his servant. And he brought forth His people with joy, and His chosen ones with gladness and singing.

Psalm 105:39-43

5. **Live with zeal and enthusiasm.**

    It's so important to enjoy every moment that we possibly can while we are alive and to live with purpose. Each step we take should have a spring in it. It's important to define our goals, fix our mind on them, and never give up until we reach them. Have you ever known someone who just wears you out from their lack of motivation? Too many people live so apathetically. They don't care if the sun comes up or if it goes down. I often wonder what causes some people to end up that way.

    Even if it had to take a cancer diagnosis, I'm grateful for the privilege of really appreciating the simple things in life that can be so easily taken for granted. I want to use all of my senses every day to the fullest—to hear, see, feel, taste and smell all the goodness that life has to offer. Now, everything means so much more to me, and I notice things that I never used to: The grass is greener, the flowers are more vivid, and now when I see a rainbow, I notice each distinct, beautiful color. Some people don't notice a rainbow when it's right before their eyes. I guess the key is looking up to see it.

    We need to put a little more *oomph* in everything we do, live our lives with gusto and some pizzazz. All it takes is just a little effort on our part to make our day more special and maybe someone else's, as well. We must develop a passion for living. Even after having cancer, we can get that back in time. We can do it!

6. **Never take one single day for granted, and have a thankful heart.** Learn to appreciate each season of your life, no matter how trivial, because it is a time of your life that will never return. No matter what you're going through, there's always something good to be found in it or a lesson to be learned. Learn to capture each moment like a priceless treasure. In everything, give thanks. Don't take anyone or anything for granted.

   We need to be more aware of our world around us. From the moment we wake up in the morning until we fall asleep at night, there are countless blessings all around us. We need to develop the habit of worshipping God in everything. Let praise be continually in our hearts for the goodness of God and all he does to sustain us each and every day. God dwells among the praises of his people. I believe that when our hearts have an attitude of gratitude, good things are more likely to come our way.

   I honestly believe that heaven is more about worship than anything else. We might as well start practicing while we're still here on earth. Do you want to know that God is with you and that he hears your prayers? Start worshipping him today with a thankful heart. He is never far away when we have a heart that is reverent and full of praise and worship. God is love. He desires our worship and praise, which creates freedom and joy. The joy of the Lord is our strength. God loves us so much that when we think we're doing something for him when we worship, he turns it back around and gives us joy unspeakable and blesses us back instead.

7. **Don't get mad over small things.**

   Since I've been through this difficult time in my life, I've learned not to sweat the small stuff. After a cancer diagnosis, everything is pretty much small stuff, don't you think? Anymore, when I'm at the mall, for example, and someone is rude or when I'm driving and another driver does something that's not courteous, I just look at them in amazement as I'm thinking, "Are you for real?" I almost feel sorry for them that they are so shallow. They must not appreciate what they already have, and they don't even know it. So many people overreact to the most bizarre things, half of which aren't really that important. It's no wonder that so many people are on blood pressure medication.

I've learned to cut the other guy some slack. For example, when traffic is slow or someone pulls in front of me, the girl at McDonald's forgets part of my order, or any other of the myriad possibilities that can go wrong, I just take it all in stride, realizing that we're all human. I certainly make my own share of mistakes and other people are apt to as well. Like the old saying, "That's why they put erasers on pencils." I just let it go, and move on. And a sense of humor can do wonders as getting upset won't change a thing.

Dealing with cancer definitely brings your priorities under careful scrutiny and puts them in their proper perspective. If things aren't going my way, I've learned to just let it go, and move on to Plan B.

8. **Learn to see life through the eyes of a child.**

(A beautiful picture that Savannah drew for my book)

This is easy to write about because I love children so much! Because everything is so new to them, they are in awe of the world around them. Have you ever noticed how down-to-earth, innocent, and trusting children are? They are just who they are. That's probably why Jesus said that we must come to him as a little child, because they already trust. Because their spirits are so innocent, faith is easy for children, whereas we adults try to figure everything out. We insist upon seeing the logic in order to believe anything.

Children live life so carefree. Spend just a short time with a child and it will change your whole viewpoint on life and for the better. To them, life is forever. They don't worry about tomorrow. They just live one day at a time. How nice if we adults could be more like them We should stop everything for one entire day and sit down and read to them, bake cupcakes, or go outside and make a snowman. We would relieve ourselves of so much anxiety by kicking back a little more often.

No matter what else we can learn from them, children can teach us to laugh. I have a special memory of my little Savannah that I will cherish forever. When we first got our Old English sheepdog, Maggie, Savannah performed one of the sweetest acts of love and kindness that only a little child is capable of. She has a special doll that she has always loved, Strawberry Shortcake, since before she could walk. Strawberry Shortcake, or Strawberry, as Savannah calls her, has been everywhere. She's had her head sewn back on numerous times and has had many trips through the washing machine. Since she is bigger than Savannah, you can always see Strawberry coming and know that Savannah is following with that little arm around Strawberry's tattered neck. Since she loves this doll so much, I bought her another one that is almost identical, thinking that in the event that something happens to Strawberry, she would have a backup. Not on your life! Although the dolls look alike and Savannah loves them both (she named the new one Cake), Strawberry just cannot be replaced.

One night, Savannah spent the night with me. When I woke up, I had to look twice. Savannah had given Maggie her beloved Strawberry, and she was sleeping angelically with Cake. Mere words could never fully describe that act of true love, which was the purest form, straight from a child's heart. It's truly a miracle that Maggie didn't chew up that doll. As if she sensing how special Strawberry was, Maggie was all snuggled up to her like Savannah always does.

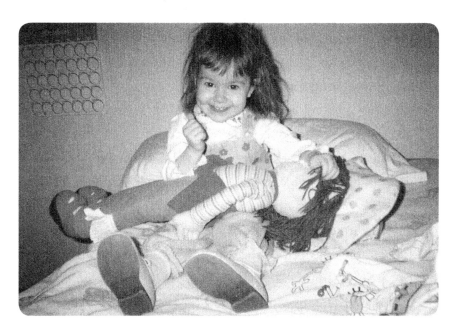

Another memory I have stamped indelibly on my heart, is a special day that Savannah and I spent together at the park, just the two of us. She was having so much fun riding the sliding board and the swings that she loves. She would run as fast as she could, jump into my arms, and I would swing her around with her giggling almost uncontrollably. Then I would chase after her, and she would hide.

All at once, I heard her little voice calling to me. "Look what I have for you Ma Ma!" She was smiling from ear to ear, showing off her dimples, and her big, beautiful, brown eyes shined with excitement. Running toward me as fast as her little legs could go, I noticed she was holding something behind her back. She then pulled out a big bouquet of dandelions, tightly clasped in her tiny hand. They were just for me! I took them home and put them in a vase on display for the whole world to see. How do you tell a child that a dandelion is just a weed? You don't! I couldn't have loved them more if they were a dozen yellow roses!

Scripture:

But Jesus called them to Him, saying, Allow the little children to come to Me, and do not hinder them, for to such as these belongs the kingdom of God.

Luke 18:16

(Just hangin out on a Saturday afternoon)

(All dressed up in their matching Easter clothes)

(I love those blonde curls!)

An Ordinary Day in the Life of a Child

As I ponder over the day at hand, I realize the average day of a child is so much more different than that of an adult. A child's day is so uncomplicated and simple.

While I'm hurrying as fast as I can to gulp down my morning toast and coffee so that I can be on time for work, my child doesn't have a care in the world. All time seems to stand still as he doodles in his cereal and giggles at the neighbor's cat outside our kitchen window.

When running errands on a trip to the grocery store, I'm racing to be first in line at the checkout, but not my child. He is busy waving to everyone he sees, and saying, "Hi!" to everyone who passes by. He has never met a stranger. He thinks everyone is his friend, and that we are all just one big happy family.

When at home doing household chores, I'm rushing about trying to catch up on laundry. My little boy is pretending to be Superman. His possibilities are endless, as he realizes he can become anyone he wants to be.

When outside raking leaves, my little boy runs and jumps into my nice neat pile, laughing sweetly, while capturing his ornery side, like only he can do. He doesn't know how much hard work was involved. All he notices is how much fun it is to hide under the newly fallen crisp autumn leaves. He doesn't have a care in the world. I'm so glad that he still has that childhood innocence so untouched by the cares that life seems to pile on us as we get older. I wish I could be more like him.

I start to mow the lawn, while complaining at how the dandelions are taking over my yard, until my little boy taps me on the back, and hands me a surprise bouquet of dandelions that he picked just for me! All of a sudden, they don't look like weeds, anymore, but my little boy's opportunity to make me happy and bring a smile to my face.

When evening draws near, I am tired from my busy, stressful day, and I can't wait to go inside and collapse into my comfy chair. All at once, I hear a lot of noise, and I look up. It's my little boy and his friends. They have a caravan of their own going on. They are part of a neighborhood parade going down the sidewalk. It's quite a commotion. They have wagons, bicycles, scooters, and rollerblades. Some of them even have their dogs in on the fun. They're going on a pretend journey. They call to me, "Do I want to go with them?" "Sure, why not?" I reply. We end up down the street at the neighborhood park. We spend the last bit of the evening chasing one another through all of the trails, and endless piles of leaves. I can't help but notice the carefree way the kids interact with one another. It's all just so natural for them, with no effort, whatsoever. Today is all that matters to them. Oh, to be a kid again, even for just one day!

We finally start back down the sidewalk, leading back to our house. I notice my little boy has captured a baby frog. It has caught his full attention. He has to jump in each and every mud puddle all the way home. He doesn't miss one. The kids start to have a contest on who can catch the most lightening bugs.

Once back home, the next thing on our agenda is a nice warm bubble bath, a bed night snack, and we kneel for a bed night prayer. We pray for our puppy, our neighbors, family members, and all of the people in the world, even in Africa. I give lots of hugs and kisses, and that final glass of water. Before I go to bed, I quietly reflect on my little boy's busy day. It was a child's paradise of endless possibilities. I quietly sneak back into his room to check on him, and look at him, lovingly, in all of that childhood innocence. He is so still, quietly sleeping, with dreams of the man in the moon, and twinkle twinkle little star. His small body is resting so angelic, with a single blonde curl that lies in a ringlet on his forehead. I look down and can't help but notice that he is holding SpongeBob tightly in one hand, and his fists, tightly clenched. I reach for his small hand, and see that he is holding two small pebbles, and a tiny leaf. They were his treasures for the day. This is just one day in the life of my little boy. He will, soon, be waking to do it all over again. I kneel down and kiss him on that precious chubby cheek and thank God for entrusting me with someone so special. What a miracle! For what was an average day in my child's life, was an amazing blessing in mine!

Life is not measured by how many breaths we take, but rather, by the moments that take our breath away. I wish you bouquets of dandelions, mud puddles, days in the park, and the simple things that all of life has to offer, from a child's point of view; But, most of all, I wish you the laughter of a child!

9. **Watch how you treat others.**

I'm much more careful now how I treat other people, and I always try to understand what they might be going through. On several occasions, when I was feeling about as low as I could possibly get, the wrong person said the wrong thing, bringing my whole day down. Sometimes all it takes is some thoughtless word or deed to hurt someone else. It could be something trivial to us, but a mountain to someone else.

You never know what the stranger who passes you on the street might be dealing with in his own life. There are so many suicides these days. I often wonder what could ever be so bad that someone would take his or her own life. We shouldn't have to think twice about being kind to others and bearing other people's burdens. Even a smile might make a huge difference in someone else's life. A matter of life or death, even. Why not start today? You will be blessed for it. Proverbs 11:17 sums it up pretty well: The merciful, kind, and generous man benefits himself (for his deeds return to bless him), but he who is cruel and callous (to the wants of others) brings on himself retribution.

If you want to be healthy and happy, be kind to others. There is an old Chinese proverb that says, "Fragrance always clings to the hand that gives you roses; so why not start passing some out each day?"

10. **Learn to laugh**—*a lot*!

One of the things that has helped me on my road to recovery is that I can see humor in so many things. There's not much to laugh about when you have cancer, but when you are recuperating, let yourself laugh as much as you possibly can. Watch funny movies, make silly faces, play with your grandchildren, or pets, or do whatever it might take to laugh, no matter what you may be going through. Just lightening up can be a tremendous help, by not taking everything so serious. I truly believe that the old saying, "Laughter is the best medicine," is true.

A smile is one of our most prized possessions. It doesn't cost a dime, but it's priceless. Have you ever seen those "before and after" pictures of people? If you really study them, you will notice that in the "before" picture the person is usually looking sour, and in the "after" picture they usually have a big smile. That smile is what makes all the difference. When you feel down, you can go with the flow or get grouchy. It's a matter of how you look at things. I tried letting my frustrations out one day by using the whole frown routine, but no matter how hard I tried to look miserable, the corners of my mouth just kept turning up.

Teenagers can teach us a few things. My kids and their friends have a little thing they all say, "LOL," which means "laughing out loud." Isn't that cute? And so true. We need to laugh, out loud and hard. There's nothing like a good, old-fashioned belly laugh, the kind where you double over and that makes your sides ache. Do you remember the scene in the movie *Mary Poppins* where they all laughed so hard that they couldn't quit and ended up on the ceiling? They weren't even sure what was so funny! You've got to admit that belly laughing is contagious!

11. **Balance is key. Learn to say "no."**

We must all find balance in our everyday lives. This includes the art of gracefully saying "no" sometimes. It's so easy to become overstressed and overloaded with things that aren't that important in the scheme of things. Consistency is important to finding balance, because if we're consistent with the most important things in life and learn to prioritize, everything else will fall into place and we won't become stressed as easily. We can pick and choose all of the other less important details.

It's important to work hard and play even harder; to roll up your sleeves and really get to work, but to know when to kick back and relax. There's nothing more gratifying than a hard day's work, when you know you have done your best. You will love that feeling of accomplishment, knowing the job was done well and that you made a positive difference in someone else's day, even if it did take a lot of effort and a little sweat to achieve the end results. It is equally important to know when it's time to rest and come apart from all that hard work, to feel rejuvenated again. You will also love those carefree days, after working so hard. You will feel like it is okay to reap the well deserved benefits of fun and recreation. It's so refreshing to have a day to do *anything* you want to do. There is a time for work, church functions, kid's ballgames, meetings, school conferences, hair appointments and all of those extra errands that cut time out of your day. They are all necessary, but they can be major time stealers that can add to your stress. You also need to carve out time to simply dangle your feet in a pool of water or lay back and look at the clouds. Everything will keep going whether you do or not.

Life can be overwhelming when we are too busy, which is true for most of us anymore. We are so caught up with running from morning until night, and I'm not so sure in the right direction, either. I'm reminded of a story that I used to read to my kids when they were little. There were five brothers who all jumped into a boat and rowed as hard and fast as they could. The only problem was that they each went a different direction and ended up going nowhere. Unfortunately, this is too true for many of us, all in the name of progress—or is it? It's important to start the day out right with a good attitude. Do you have a positive outlook and wake up refreshed and ready to begin another day? Yesterday is gone. Tomorrow isn't here yet. Today is the only day that you can work with. Try starting it stress free, and with purpose. So that the moment your feet first touch the floor in the morning until the end of the day, you won't wonder, *What was this day all about?* Some days you might be behind before you get up, and you can't help but wonder if you should have stayed in bed in the first place. Everyone has a day like that now and then, but hopefully you won't have many of them.

We all need to literally stop and smell the roses. Learn to enjoy the day at hand, because tomorrow will be here before you know it. I am reminded of a funny saying I saw on a plaque, which makes me chuckle to myself on some of my more chaotic days: "I finally got it all together, but I forgot where I put it." I know that feeling all too well!

Scripture:
To everything there is a season, and a time for every matter or purpose under heaven.

Ecclesiastes 3:1

12. **Do things you enjoy.**

    I've learned how short life really is. I want to take it all in for as long as I can. I have learned to fully enjoy everything that I can, even the little, mundane things. Not too long ago, a lot of everyday things that I had to do were drudgery to me, but I've learned to appreciate the value of simple pleasures. It doesn't have to cost a lot of money. Some of life's most fun and rewarding times are inexpensive or completely free. If you have to actually sit down and make a list of things that make you happy, maybe you should. You've got nothing to lose but sheer boredom.

    If you're not used to thinking of yourself instead of everyone else, this may seem a bit hard for you at first. That was my problem, because it's easy to get into the habit of catering to everyone else so much that you forget who you even are. Thinking of your own needs is not at all selfish. It's quite the contrary. When you start enjoying your own life more, you will be much more fun to be around, and you will brighten a lot of other lives along the way.

I don't know why, but I had always wanted an Old English sheepdog. Call me crazy. Everyone else did. I think it's their soft, furry bodies that remind me of a stuffed animal. And they don't just jump; they bounce on all fours. They are a little on the hyper side—kind of like me, I guess. If you can get past all of that, sheepdogs are like great, big, loveable, teddy bears. When I saw sheepdog puppies for sale, I knew in my heart that one of them had my name on it. When I picked my puppy out, she was three weeks old. There she was, my Maggie, a three-week-old little ball of black-and-white fluff. I've been in love with her ever since, which is a good thing for her, because that has saved her during some of her not so lovable moments.

At first, everyone around me thought that I needed my thyroid medicine adjusted, especially my husband. Even so, I can't tell you how much happiness that big fur ball has brought into my life. She makes me laugh. She needs me as much as I need her. Maggie has helped me to get my eyes off my problems and to think about someone else. There's something therapeutic about being needed.

Maybe a dog is the last thing you want or need. How about volunteering at the hospital? Or taking a sick neighbor a bouquet of flowers or a bowl of soup? When you do a random act of kindness for someone else, your own soul can't help but be blessed. As you give of yourself to help someone else, it diminishes your own problems for a little while, and every little bit helps. Enjoying every day to the fullest is what counts.

Below is a list of some of my favorite things that may give you some ideas:

1. My family
2. My grandchildren, especially their laughter
3. Flowers—any and all, the more colorful the better
4. Good movies—my favorites are the ones you sit with a box of tissues or you laugh until your sides ache.
5. Roller coasters
6. A bird singing nearby
7. Good food, especially pasta, pasta, and more pasta
8. The smell of coffee in my favorite coffee mug
9. Writing
10. A beautiful sunset
11. Incredible nature
12. A fresh breeze
13. A smile from a stranger
14. A hug from a friend
15. Sunny days
16. Good music that I can dance to lifts my spirits like nothing else. My grandkids and I can really get down and do some serious jamming.
17. Going to the mall
18. Flying a kite
19. Baking cupcakes (my grandchildren, especially love decorating them with *silly* faces.)
20. My favorite Starbucks drink, Strawberry Iced Frappacino

21. Getting my hair done
22. Last, but certainly not least, riding in my Miata with the top down

Each person is different. Things that I enjoy may not make your list at all. Only you know what truly makes you happy. What makes you happy? Go find out today!

13. **Surround yourself with happy, positive people.**

This is self-explanatory, as only makes sense that the attitudes of happy people with a positive outlook will eventually rub off on you. These people make your goals seem more attainable, and they encourage you along the way. After all, that's what a friend is. They love you at all times I can't emphasize enough what an important role they play in the recovery process. We need to be around people who care about us, and who will encourage and lift us up on a regular basis.

14. **Get organized.**

You're probably wondering what this topic could possibly have to do with overcoming cancer. Getting organized may not be the number one factor on your mind, but as insignificant as it may seem, it is important. Depending on your energy level and how you feel, it's a good idea to be organized in all aspects of your life such as your health, your finances, your home, your children, and your time in general.

Getting organized improves mental clarity and will help you sift through the trivial things that rob you of your time. Let's face it, when you aren't feeling up to par, you don't want to search for an important insurance paper, for example, before you can go to the doctor. If you're organized, you can get right to whatever it is that you need, without all the hassle.

There's still hope even if you've been in a fog for awhile and have been searching for a particular item like playing "Where's Waldo?" Most of us have been there at some point, and it's not that hard to get back on track. Start with your health, your purse, then your bills, and on down the list, such as your household cleaning and bigger projects. I'd save the big ones like the garage, for example, until you are more on your feet. Baby steps can make you feel like you are making progress. Just go with the flow, and eventually, things will be back to normal.

There are a few unspoken rules to follow that will make it seem easier. The first step is to clear the clutter. Get rid of the things that are in the way and of no use to you so that you can see everything more clearly. Once you do this, it may be easier than you realized to get to the heart of the problem. Another suggestion I have is to become a list maker. Sometimes I think I'm on the paranoid side with this one, but, honestly, I don't know how I would make it without my lists. I've done this for as long as I can remember, starting when I was a child. One summer, I was so bored so I decided to make a list of all of the things that I could think of to do. I've never been bored since. There have been some chaotic days that I've wondered if it was more of a curse than a blessing, but overall lists are great! I make lists for everything, from my personal goals, to goals for my housework, family fun ideas, etc. You name the topic, and there is a potential list in the making.

What's important to you? We all need to get organized. It's a great asset to teach our children and is a good way to cultivate happy, well-adjusted, goal-oriented families.

15. **Tune out the bad things.**

We need to learn what to let in and what to tune out. I like to know what's going on in the world, but I can only watch the news for a few minutes before I end up feeling hopeless and depressed. I'm not denying that we should be informed, but there's a fine line between knowing the facts and bombarding our minds for hours on end with the same story. It's like our minds are constantly being programmed to hear these negative, worldly viewpoints until we are too depressed to get out of bed.

If you think television is bad, the radio is not any better. Before you go to bed at night, it's not a good idea to listen to everything that is wrong in the world, because when you close your eyes and fall asleep, that's the last thing that is on your mind. People wonder why they are so sad all the time and that antidepressants are the number one prescription that doctors write for their patients. Yet it's no wonder. If enough people hear so much gloom every day, their attitudes get bad, and they think, *how is anything going to get better?* Once they lose all hope—and that's basically what they are doing when they cram all that junk into their mind—it not only makes them too weary to get out of bed, but it makes each step too heavy.

I honestly believe that our attitudes play a major role in fighting off all illnesses, including cancer, so we can't afford to allow one wrong thought to invade our minds. We have to constantly filter out the junk, and let in all the good. I know things are in a mess, but my hope is not in the news, the economy, the stock market, the president, or the doctors. My hope is supremely in God and God alone. That's when you will start to experience real peace, no matter what's going on all around you. We are to renew our minds daily. I don't know about you, but I'm going to fix my thoughts on what is true, lovely, and of a good report, and let God take care of the news, because I know that he is taking care of me.

16. **Don't procrastinate.**

Some things in life are more important than others. This is where prioritizing comes in. Our families should be high on our list. If your child has a ballgame, for example, or anything that is important to them, you should be there for them and take an interest in what they are doing. There are some things that just won't wait and so many milestones our kids go through.

Also, our elderly parents need us now more than ever. They were there for us, and now it's our turn to be there for them. As they age, they are more vulnerable to accidents and illnesses. They need our attention so much at this crucial time in their lives.

Our marriages can't be put on hold either. To have a good, healthy marriage, we need to take time out each day to connect and really listen to what our spouse is saying. We all need to be heard and loved. This would prevent a lot of divorces.

We can't neglect time spent with God either. He is waiting for us to spend time with him each day in prayer. It's important to start every day with him first on our list. He wants to go through each day with us and help us make sense of everything.

Lastly, it's crucial that we don't put off time for ourselves. We need some downtime every once in awhile to regroup and get our focus back on what is most important.

All of these things contribute to the quality of our lives and to our loved ones. If you're waiting until the time is right to start enjoying life, don't. Nike's slogan is right on target: Just do it! There is never a better time to start than the present. We can't put off our health, our families, God, or ourselves. I never want to look back with regrets and wish I'd spent more time with those who are the most important to me. I can't think of anything sadder to know it's too late. Some things can wait, but people can't!

17. Develop a healthy self esteem

After you've had cancer, there's something you are left to deal with besides your health: your self-esteem. Once you've been through all the tests, surgery, treatments, and whatever else you have to go through, such as the emotional trauma, there is an uncertainty that hangs over you like a fog. It is lurking all around you. This uncertainty comes from the fragments of feelings that you are trying to make some sense of like pieces of a jigsaw puzzle that you haven't been able to put together yet. If you are like most cancer patients, you probably have a scar. If you don't have a physical scar, then most certainly you have some emotional scars that are hidden under the surface, which are sometimes harder to heal than the physical ones. You might have lost your hair or your breasts; maybe you had a tracheotomy or lost or gained a lot of weight. There could be any number of other noticeable changes for the world to see.

Through all of this, try to get the proper perspective. The main thing is to be thankful. You're still here! How awesome! The road may have been long and rough, but you've come this far. With your second chance, you can always work with all those other nuisances you have to deal with that don't have to determine who you are. You are still the same person that you were before the diagnosis. You still have that beautiful spirit within you. That old saying, "What's inside is what counts," has a lot of truth in it. It may take you a little while to find yourself again, but you can do it. I know you can.

As difficult as this has been for me, I'm still grateful because it has changed me completely and for the better. I have learned so much more about God, people, life, and about myself. I discovered inner strengths that I didn't know I had. Our true strengths come from the inside, and soon they will radiate to the outside. Cancer isn't the beginning nor is it the end. Cancer doesn't define who I am as a woman. Its how I've learned to cope with cancer that counts. If I can get past that and not give up, cancer cannot defeat me.

Yes, there can be life after cancer. Get your class back. Take a deep breath. Square your shoulders. Stand up tall. Put one foot in front of the other and give that winning smile that is uniquely yours. Put that sparkle back in your eyes and move forward with confidence, knowing and believing that better days are in front of you and that you can be the best person that you were meant to be. You are so special! There is nobody else like you!

18. **Never give up. Fight the good fight.**

People give up so easily. They give up on their marriages, their families, themselves, their health, and even God. Many people want instant satisfaction, but we all know that good things comes to those who are willing to wait. We are building on a false hope when we refuse to wait and when we are not willing to fight for whatever it is that we are striving for. In time, with a little faith and perseverance, we will reap the fruits of our labor.

When fighting cancer, the last thing anyone should do is to give up. Dig in your heels, and fight the good fight! Keep on pressing on. If you feel like giving up, and we all do at times, just get back up, and keep moving toward your goal. Fight cancer with all you have in you. It's not always what happens to us that determines the quality of life or the outcome, but rather the way we respond to the situation. What we do with what we have is what makes the difference. Start where you are. Each small effort will become a ripple effect that starts where you are and will expand into all other areas of your life. Anything you do to improve your overall mental and physical health will influence your future for the better. Don't ever forget: When the music stops, you need to keep on dancing like never before!

19. **Don't compare yourself to others.**

Each of us is unique with distinct qualities, gifts, and talents. No one can be you like you can. But it's easy to fall into the habit of comparing ourselves with others.

When I was first diagnosed with cancer, I compared my case with other cancer patients' cases. I soon learned, however, that cancer affects each person differently. I remember sitting in many doctor's offices and seeing all of those people who were waiting like I was. Some of their bodies were ravaged with cancer, but others seemed to beat it against unimaginable odds. Each person responds differently to treatment; what may not work for one person may work well for another.

The best advice that I can give is to follow your doctor's orders and follow his or her course of treatment. Try not to pay too much attention to what everyone else says because they all have a different idea. The path is different for each person, and the fear of the unknown leaves you feeling powerless, especially in the beginning when you can't see the full picture of what lies ahead. Try not to focus on the negatives, but instead focus on the positive things you can do to improve your situation.

Just be yourself, and believe in yourself. Learn to celebrate *your* strengths and successes. You have so much to offer to those you love and to the world, so don't compare yourself to anyone else. God gave you the ability to make a difference, because no one else is just like you. Make each day count.

20. **Learn to forgive.**

Many of these topics that I've addressed so far may not seem to have a lot to do with cancer, but, as I've stressed numerous times before, I am a firm believer that our attitudes and emotions have much more to do with our physical health than most people realize.

I can't stress enough the importance of forgiveness. Forgiving someone who has hurt us frees us to let go and concentrate on positive things so that we can direct our prayers and energy into getting well. Let's face it. We've all been hurt, and most of us are guilty of hurting someone else although maybe not intentionally. When there's nothing we can do to change what someone has done to hurt us, there's something we can do: let it go. Holding onto bitterness and resentment opens the door to unnecessary stress that can lower our immune system, which can lead to many illnesses, including cancer, heart attacks, and a number of other health issues, such as stomach problems, high blood pressure, stroke and depression. This can ultimately turn into mental illness. What we hold inside can drastically affect our physical bodies. If God can forgive us when we're so undeserving, we should be able to forgive others.

You may have been hurt so badly that you're not sure how you could ever recover. You need to release that hurt to God as there is no hurt that God's love cannot heal. It may take time, but for all the good it does, you will be so glad you did. Of course, your health will be affected because you are letting go of all that poison inside of you. You will, then, be set free from the bondage that has enslaved you for so long. Do you remember that saying, *Let Go and Let God*. This is so true. You can't do it, but **He Can!** God gives us the grace to deal with every problem that we face, one day at a time.

Try this simple remedy. Take a bouquet of balloons outside, and let them go. As you release them, believe that you are releasing all of the hurt and anger you are holding inside from the past. Take a deep breath, and start with a clean slate. Breathe out the old attitudes, and breathe in a fresh new beginning. Holding in your hurts wounds you more than it wounds the person who hurt you.

Forgiveness is twofold. As you relinquish your pain to God, your soul will be blessed, and the healing process will begin emotionally, spiritually, and physically.

21. **Enjoy nature.**

Nature is a natural healer. Fresh air has air conditioning beat; there's nothing more refreshing than a gentle breeze blowing softly across your face. I love to enjoy the flowers and walk barefoot in the grass. I love to hear a bird singing in the distance as she prepares her nest for her new babies to hatch. I love baby bunnies as they scurry across my backyard, and there's nothing like watching a deer prancing through the forest to attend to her young. I love to awaken to the sound of the morning dove in the peaceful serenity of a brand-new day. Before I close my eyes at night, I love gazing at the starry sky and looking for the Big Dipper as crickets chirp a midnight serenade. I love hearing the giant oak tree whipping its branches back and forth as a storm approaches. And I'm always amazed at the intensity of loud thunder that lets me know that someone bigger than all of us is still in control.

If you stop long enough and pay attention, you will realize that nature goes on all by itself and on a perfect schedule. I love the spring. No matter how long or short the winter has been, I love those first sounds of new life everywhere. There is something holy as the whole world comes alive once again, and the once harsh, bone-chilling wind of winter becomes the gentle, warm breeze of spring. Even the rain is welcome, because I know it will produce the rich, vibrant green grass and trees. I still enjoy running, carefree as a child through the rain, while birds sing everywhere in their own heavenly chorus as they flit joyfully from tree to tree.

I am always excited to see the flower bulbs poking through the ground that will soon be those colorful tulips and daffodils that I envisioned when I planted them on that cold, fall afternoon. Buds appearing on the trees as their beautiful blossoms start to unfold such magnificent colors fills me with anticipation.

Everything is fresh and new each year; a new season, and a new chance. I believe it can be that way in our lives, too. What was once dead and lifeless can become fresh and new. Go ahead. Give God, yourself, and nature a chance to transform you into that beautiful butterfly that is just waiting to be set free!

Scripture:
O Lord, how many and varied are Your works! In wisdom have You made them all; the earth is full of your riches and your creatures.

Psalm 104:24

22. **Make each day a celebration.**

Each day is a gift from God where we are given another chance to start all over again. For this very reason, every day is cause for celebration.

First, we need to know what a celebration is, and then what it is we are celebrating. Here are many words that define what a celebration is to me: happiness, joy, jubilation, festivity, and the Spanish word fiesta that means party.

Now that we know what a celebration is, what is it that we are celebrating? There are many good reasons why we should celebrate or rejoice: God, our families and friends, our country and freedom, our victories, our accomplishments, and definitely, our good health. Life in itself is a celebration, and we need to celebrate the lives we touch every day. No one is insignificant in the eyes of God. From the President of the United States to the beggar on the street, everyone has worth with a role to play and the duty to contribute something to the world. Each person can leave a lasting impression upon those they meet. As no two snowflakes are alike, no two people are alike. We each have something valuable to offer.

Okay, now that we know all about celebrating, let's throw a party! Get out the noisemakers and the party hats! Let's be glad and shout with all our might! Let's sound the trumpet, shake the tambourines, strike up the band, and clash the cymbals! Let's dance, be merry, have a feast, and don't forget the fireworks! Like a family reunion gone wild.

One of the many ways that I love to celebrate is to enjoy my family and acknowledge each person's worth. Each person that I know and love holds a different and lasting place in my heart. They are each like a beautiful jewel that, when put all together, makes up a beautiful crown.

My children are all different, but each one is priceless in their own way. There are little things about each one of them that make them who they are, and I know the simple, little things that are meaningful to them. When they come home, I like to add that extra touch that makes them feel loved and tells them that they have a special place in our family.

Holidays and family traditions are also a wonderful way to celebrate. One of our family's favorite holidays is Thanksgiving. Although, Uncle Brent's turkey and stuffing, Mom's sweet potatoes and deviled eggs, Grandma's mashed potatoes and gravy, and Sarah and Beth's pumpkin pie are all great, that's not what makes the day. It's all the family members taking one day to gather together to enjoy our special family traditions and to reconnect with one another combined with Grandma's wisdom, Mom's love, Dad's sense of humor, and all the kids' laughter. That's really the true heart of any holiday.

No matter how busy we are, or what else is going on, we should always take the time to celebrate those we love. In my opinion, they are our God given joys that make this life so wonderful. There's a special couple I have known for a long time. On their last anniversary, the husband bought his wife, who has had Alzheimer's for several years, a dozen red roses. When he brought them home to her, he hugged and kissed her like it was their first anniversary. He was celebrating his love for her and their marriage of many years. Although she can't remember, he will never forget.

As this book is nearing its completion, the Fourth of July is just around the corner. This is one of the top holidays that we, Americans like to celebrate not only for our families, because of the usual traditions, of the backyard barbecues, homemade ice cream, and of course the fireworks, but for our nation as well. The blessed United States of America! I know much has gone wrong, but patriotism still rocks! Francis Scott Key was inspired to write our beloved national anthem, "The Star-Spangled Banner," but it wasn't written beneath sunny skies in the middle of the day, On the contrary. It was written on a rainy night under dark skies or what I might refer to as Francis Scott Key's midnight hour as he witnessed the bombardment of Fort McHenry in the War of 1812. This great patriotic song was born as the rockets flew overhead and the dark sky lit up with fire. When early dawn was visible, not only did Key have cause to celebrate, but our entire nation celebrated as we had won the victory. Our flag was flying high in the sky. The battle was won!

Last, but most importantly, I want to celebrate my God! Without him, there would be nothing to celebrate. He can turn the most ordinary day into a party with much rejoicing and celebrating. Do you have a battle raging in your life? Are you so weak and tired that you don't feel like celebrating? Do you feel like you've been shipwrecked on a deserted island in your midnight hour? Cheer up! There is always something to celebrate no matter how insignificant it might seem. Each baby step in the right direction is a reason to celebrate. When you can't see the light at the end of the tunnel, Jesus becomes the light *in* the tunnel.

The next time you hear the rockets soaring, start celebrating your victory. Hang your own flag high. Lift it proud for the whole world to see. Rejoice and be glad, and remember: *His banner over you is love!*

Scripture:
He brought me to the banqueting house, and his banner over me was love (for love waved as a protecting and comforting banner over my head when I was near him).

Song of Solomon 2:4

After all that, it's only right to include our national anthem! I always get a tear in my eye and cold chills when I hear it! God Bless America!

The Star-Spangled Banner

What so proudly we hailed at the twilight's last gleaming?
Whose broad stripes and bright stars thru the perilous fight,
O'er the ramparts we watched were so gallantly streaming?
And the rocket's red glare, the bombs bursting in air,
Gave proof through the night that our flag was still there.
O, say does that star-spangled banner yet wave
O'er the land of the free and the home of the brave?

23. **You can get fit and healthy again.**

This topic requires a chapter of its own. (Chapter Fifteen)

Scripture:
The light in the eyes (of him whose heart is joyful) rejoices the hearts of others, and good news nourishes the bones.
Proverbs 15: 30

A special note:

All these things I've mentioned may sound great, but they're not always easy to do. Fighting cancer or some other illness may seem like an uphill climb, and the first step is always the hardest. You will find that as you continue to work on these areas, by incorporating healthy attitudes, along with pursuing fitness and health, it will get easier with time.

Chapter Fifteen

You Can Get Fit and Healthy Again

When I was going through the surgery and radiation, my body was totally drained. Some people who I've talked to were able to whizz through without much difficulty, but that is hardly the norm. Most people I've spoken with said that it was a very rough time for them. As I emphasized earlier, everyone is different.

I spent many days in bed for about the first three months. That much-needed rest was good for me at the time and essential in the healing process. But during the long, hard days of recovery, it's easy to get discouraged and feel like you'll never be back to your old self again. Try to be patient. Your strength will eventually return. I still have days that I don't feel as well as I would like. I get tired more easily than I ever have in my life.

Since I've been treated, am cancer-free, and on the correct dose of thyroid medication, I feel better than I have in a long time. My body is starting to feel normal again, although it's hard to define what normal is anymore. There are many ups and downs, especially during the first year until the medicine is adjusted correctly. On my sluggish days, I'm still grateful when I consider the alternative if they hadn't caught the cancer in time.

Menopausal symptoms don't make it any easier. When hot flashes quit flashing and turn into one long flash, it can be irritating, to say the least. Menopause and cancer don't mix. Talk about drama!

As my energy gradually improved, I wanted more than anything to have the endurance that I once had and more of it. I know it's dramatic, but I envisioned myself with boundless energy like the movie, *Son of Flubber*. I pictured myself riding for miles on a bicycle, jumping on a trampoline and even pole-vaulting high in the air over our house. Although, I've never pole-vaulted in my life, it looks like fun. Hey, I can dream, can't I? It was a good mental picture for me at the time.

I finally got the motivation to be as fit and healthy as possible. I've never done anything halfway in my life; I wanted to go all out and be healthier than I'd ever been in my life. It's either all or nothing!

I believe that our attitudes have a huge impact on us and affect our health for good or bad. As much as I wanted to do all those things I envisioned, I knew that it would be a major achievement to just get out of bed on some days. I knew I was in for the fight of my life!

This was something I had to do on my own. You know, like people in the Olympics are going for the gold medal, the ultimate prize? I knew that it would take everything within me to achieve my dream. I knew it wouldn't be easy, but I laugh at conflict! I can be the world's most stubborn woman once I make up my mind. Just ask my husband.

While I was recovering, I made up my mind that when I felt like it, I would get as fit and healthy as possible. Several months later, I entered an essay contest and won a fitness consultation with Denise Austin, a well-known fitness expert, which was just the boost I needed to get motivated. I knew it was time to roll up my sleeves and get serious. I said, "I can do this. Watch out world!"

Below is a list of healthy tips that I am trying to incorporate into my daily routine. You may find some of them beneficial also:

- Having a good attitude is extremely important. Staying positive really helps as does being around as many positive people as possible.
- I am trying to keep my weight off. I have a few pounds to go, but it's important to stay as active as you can to boost your metabolism.
- I try to work out five days a week for thirty minutes. This includes cardio, flexibility, and strength training. I try to do strength training at least two times a week, resting one day between workouts. Strength training helps to strengthen our muscles. Cardio fights heart disease, which is a major killer in women. Good examples of this type of exercise are walking, running, bicycling, kickboxing, or swimming; basically, any exercise that will get within your target heart rate. Flexibility, or stretching, loosens you up and helps to avoid the pain and stiffness of simply moving, that so many of us have as we age. It also helps fight arthritis pain and its symptoms. Sometimes all it takes is a sneeze or turning our body the wrong way to end up in bed for a week with a bad back. This can happen if our muscles are weak or out of shape. Stretching and flexibility help to make our bodies more flexible and not so weak and stiff. I've had back spasms, and I don't even want to go there. All I can

say is that I've had three kids and that wasn't as painful. A bad back can bring a big man to his knees in tears. Another benefit of exercise is that it can improve your balance. Your workout can be as simple as you would like it to be or as elaborate as a fancy gym. The main thing is to get moving. I usually do my work out right at home. I pop in an exercise DVD, and I'm all set. Wear comfortable clothing. There are many useful types of exercise equipment to help you in your quest for better health. Some of them might include: an exercise mat, free weights, (three and five pounds), a stepper for aerobics, a stationary bike, a mini trampoline, a treadmill, even an elliptical machine. The more variety you have, the less bored you will become. Swimming is also a very good form of exercise. I also like kickboxing. We all have our own individual preferences. When you feel better, you might want to test your own endurance by trying out for a marathon or going online to the Presidents Challenge website where you can get an evaluation of your fitness level. This is a program that encourages Americans to become more active in their everyday lives. Exercise can also help battle cancer-related fatigue. Many cancer survivors report a loss of energy after treatment, which leads to a lower quality of life.

These are some of the ways that exercise can benefit a cancer survivor:

1. Reduces pain and nausea
2. Improves cardiovascular endurance and muscular strength

3. Reduces fatigue
4. Reduces anxiety
5. Encourages the survivor to change their focus from being ill to staying well

- I wear a pedometer and shoot for the recommended 10,000 steps a day.
- I try to stay as active as possible, even on the weekends. Just taking my grandchildren to the park is a workout! It's just as important for them to keep active also.

Suggestions for improving your overall health:

- Here are the vitamins I take daily. Before you start a daily vitamin regimen, consult with your doctor.
    1. A multivitamin
    2. Calcium, at least 500 mg daily, especially after menopause to help prevent osteoporosis
    3. Fish Oil 1200 mg daily
    4. Vitamin C 500 mg daily
    5. Super B Complex 1 tablet daily

- I try to get at least eight hours of sleep each night. A nice bubble bath can help you to relax if you're having trouble falling asleep.
- I drink at least eight glasses of water daily. It's good for your skin, prevents dehydration, and keeps your body running smoothly. I love water. I believe it is the healthiest drink there is.

- I try to eat as healthy as possible. I love yogurt, fruits, veggies, whole grains, and lean meats. I don't eliminate any food group, and I eat a variety of healthy foods to replenish my body with all the nutrients it needs. I try not to drink too much soda pop, as it's loaded with sugar and empty calories that will go nowhere but on your hips. My grandma used to say, "Honey, my waistline is a thing of the past." It doesn't have to be that way, and, yes, I do love chocolate and adore ice cream. They are my weaknesses. I try not to indulge too often, but everyone needs a little treat sometimes. Life is too short to not enjoy the things we love, as long as we don't make it a daily habit.
- I love the sunshine. It's so refreshing to take a long walk on a sunny day. Just don't forget the sun block. I try to use an SPF of at least 15 or higher and avoid tanning beds altogether. A bronzed body is beautiful at the time, but it can lead to premature aging and even skin cancer down the road. We don't need that! Self-tanners might not look as natural as the real thing, but they are worth it.
- I love my coffee, but overdoing it makes me jittery.
- I try to keep everything as natural as possible. I try to avoid taking too many different medicines. Important prescriptions can't be helped if you have to take them. I take Tylenol as a last resort, but I try to do everything natural first to see if that works. People take too many over-the-counter medicines. If you look at the labels, some of them can be very dangerous. You could also have a dangerous drug interaction and end up with more trouble than you started with in the first place. You should also talk to your

doctor before taking certain vitamins and herbs, because they can also be dangerous.

- I take good care of my teeth and floss daily. I believe that a healthy smile is priceless. Do you want to whiten your teeth, naturally? Those expensive teeth-whitening products are helpful, but a natural way to do it is to eat healthy. Cut out sugary drinks and desserts. Mama was right. Eat your carrot sticks. It's a known fact that eating healthy, including fruits and veggies in your diet, and drinking plenty of water, will enhance your smile and the overall appearance of those pearly whites.
- A good beauty regimen is important for your health as well as your self-esteem.
- I use a moisturizer daily, as one of the symptoms of thyroid trouble can be itchy, dry skin, and hair loss.
- A good haircut may be just what your hair needs to make it feel full and thick again, and to enhance its natural shine. This will help restore the health of your hair. I also usually let my hair dry naturally as much as possible. Hair dryers can really dry out your hair.
- It's very important to keep all of your regularly scheduled doctor appointments, especially now more than ever. Keep your annual physicals, mammograms, pap smears, dental appointments, etc.
- Green tea is a healthy drink. It contains antioxidants, which will help your body to protect itself against free-radicals, or molecules, that can damage cells.
- Try not to skip meals. I eat three meals a day and two snacks. Breakfast is the most important meal of the day. It helps you start the day right, so you will avoid that mid-

morning slump. It doesn't have to be an enormous meal to be healthy.
- Try to avoid fast food restaurants as much as possible. When you have no other choice, try to stick with something on the healthier side of the menu.
- Try to avoid stress.
- And whatever you do, don't smoke!

Many needless health concerns could be avoided with a little self discipline each day by working on these areas. Start slowly and work your way into it. Don't overdo it. Drink plenty of water so you don't get dehydrated. Good health and a radiant complexion can't be bought, no matter how much money you spend. It doesn't come from a bottle. It starts on the inside and radiates to the outside. Try a few of these ideas. You will start to benefit in every area and will notice that you have that healthy all-American-girl look. We all have those days when we put on a sloppy tee shirt, pull our hair up into a ponytail, and wear no makeup at all. But even on those days, you will look great, because you are feeling good from the inside out.

I know all of this information is quite a bit to absorb all at once. Start small. Make an effort to try something new each day and stick with it. You will be glad you did. Set your goals and reward your accomplishments. You'll be better for it.

This chapter has been a lot about fighting, but in a good way. We need to fight for our families, fight for our faith, and fight for our health. Nothing worth pursuing ever comes easy. Sometimes the harder you try the more opposition you seem to have. This isn't the time to lie down and give up. Get some spunk and fight. Your very life depends on it!

Scripture:

<u>Yet amid all these things we are more than conquerors and gain a surpassing victory through Him Who loved us.</u>
Romans 8:37

Chapter Sixteen

Keep Looking for Your Rainbow

After the storm, there is a rainbow, and calm is restored once again. That's how I look at my experience with thyroid cancer. The Bible says that weeping may endure for a night, but joy comes in the morning! Psalm 30:5 For His anger is but for a moment, but his favor is for a lifetime. Weeping may endure for a night, but joy comes in the morning.

Have you ever really looked at a rainbow? When the lightning flashes, and the thunder rolls, if you look up at just the right time, there is the rainbow in all its glory. They are so full of color as that stream of light bursts through from heaven at just the right moment. No matter how dark the surrounding clouds are, there is a glimmer of renewed hope.

You may feel as though you have been tossed about in your own dark storm for quite awhile. You may think it's too dark and that you will never see the light again. But don't lose hope. When you least expect it, little colors will start appearing until your rainbow is in full color for the whole world to see. You will burst forth with renewed hope that you are going to overcome all of the things that have been pulling you down for so long. Only this time, you will have a new song to sing—a song of hope. You will be stronger than you ever believed possible!

God is holding every tear that you've shed in the palm of his hand. He knows what he's doing and has everything under control, according to his perfect timing. When the time is right, he will turn all those tears into a glorious rainbow. You will then know what true rejoicing is!

Sometimes things don't work out as you want. Sometimes the medical report is not so good. During those times, you need to cast your cares on God, because he cares for you. He will bring you through the storm ever so gently. If you don't see the rainbow now, it's certain that you will see it on the other side of the pain you must endure in this moment. One day God will make all things new and all of this present suffering will be worth one glorious day in heaven.

Scripture:

For God so loved the world that he gave his one and only son, that whoever believes in him shall not perish but have eternal life.

John 3:16 NIV

Chapter Seventeen

An Update

Many things have changed during the course of my writing this book. Last fall, I had a little scare when my thyroglobulin was elevated. Thyroglobulin is used as a tumor marker, because increased levels in the blood is a sign of a possible cancer recurrence, because thyroglobulin is not supposed to show up once you've had your thyroid removed. So, I had to have an ultrasound of my lymph nodes, which turned out okay. I am still cancer-free. I have so much to be thankful for.

I still have to go to the doctor every three or four months to be checked. The follow up tests are an ongoing thing. The longer you go without a recurrence, the better the prognosis. My life has been busy and very full ever since the last ultrasound.

My younger daughter, Bethany, got married while I've been writing this book. She had a winter wedding, which took place one week before Christmas. I thought I was busy for Sarah's wedding, but I had no idea what a Christmas wedding would be like. Not only was I working on the wedding plans, I was baking cookies and

Christmas shopping. What a wild and crazy time! Between singing "Deck the Halls" and "Rudolph the Red-Nosed Reindeer," I was up all night making cookies and fudge and wrapping presents. I would fall into bed in the wee hours of the morning, only to wake up and run off to work a couple hours after my head hit the pillow. Talk about running on adrenalin! I wouldn't advise anyone to make a habit of that lifestyle, but I was having so much fun! It sure beat going through radiation and isolation at Christmas like I did two years ago.

During all of the madness, I could hear God calling me away long enough to speak peace into my day. I could hear him reminding me of the reason for Christmas and life in general. It was as if he was saying, "Take a deep breath, and close your eyes. Hold tightly to my hand. You're in for the ride of your life, but if you don't let go of my hand, I'll get you through it!"

The day of the beautiful Victorian wedding finally arrived. Unlike Sarah's spring afternoon wedding, Bethany's winter evening wedding was romantic and lit by candlelight. It was a fairy tale wedding. The church was adorned with hurricane lanterns, white roses, and gorgeous white pew bows. Bethany wore my wedding gown that I married her father in thirty years ago. I was so honored. It had a large hoop underneath and stood out full. The gown was adorned with Venice lace with a long train. As the ushers unrolled the aisle runner, I saw Bethany waiting. She looked like a princess. Not only was she my baby girl, she was Josh's beautiful bride. Josh is a wonderful addition to our family. We all love him.

Of course, I cried at her wedding, but it was even harder the day she came home to clean out her room and pack her things to move out. As I helped her carry the last load to her car, it hit me. I always knew that noisy, cluttered room would someday be vacant.

But all of a sudden, it seemed so final. One memory, after another, unfolded in my mind. How did she go from being that little girl, playing with her Barbie dolls, to now a grown woman? Her teenage years nearly drove me crazy! She looked so cute in her braces, even if she did hate them. I'll never forget those endless piles of laundry she created. That girl could go through the clothes! I hated that deafening music and her teenage tantrums, as everything was a crisis to her. She was a true teenage drama queen. I can still hear her bedroom door slam shut after she hung that "KEEP OUT!" sign.

I thought it would never end, but it did, and my heart is breaking! Now I feel like putting my own "KEEP OUT!" sign on that door. I can't go back in there until my heart stops aching. I'm sure that in time I will heal, but for now, I hurt. That room won't always seem so empty and will have purpose once again. I can almost see her children playing in there someday, just like she did. I've earned these tears, so for now I'm going to allow myself to reminisce, even if it's just for today.

(Mark and I giving Bethany a Congratulation Kiss after the wedding)

This book has been so long in the making that I have more news to share with you. I have a new grandson, baby Jackson, Bethany and Josh's son. He was born three months early, weighing in at slightly less than two pounds. He was in the neonatal intensive care unit for three months after he was born. The only contact Bethany and Josh had with him those first few days after his birth was to put their hand in the incubator to touch him. He reinvented the word "preemie"! As small as he was, he was perfectly formed and had a full head of dark hair. It was a very trying time for our family, but once again, God had his hand on baby Jackson. He is another book entirely, but all I will say now is that he is another reminder of God's miracle-working power and amazing love in our lives.

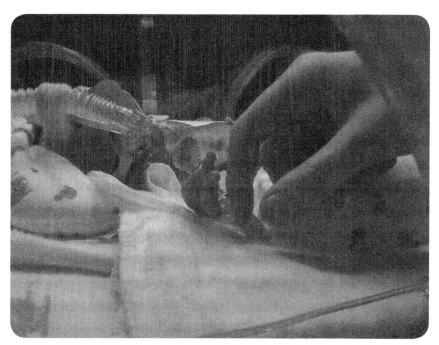

(In the incubator in the Neonatal Intensive Care Unit at Nationwide Children's Hospital . . . Reaching for his mommy's hand)

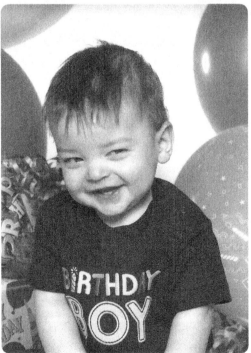

(What a blessing he has been to us!)

Bethany's life isn't the only one that is changing. Travis just graduated from high school a few months ago. He has grown so tall and was so handsome in his cap and gown. If I could just hold onto him a little longer and not let him go; after all, he's my youngest, my baby. I loved watching him play baseball when he was little. I was his biggest fan! He was so cute when he got his first home run. I'll never forget watching him run as fast as he could with those little wobbly knees. He was so cute wearing his ball cap, and those toothless smiles are unforgettable.

(My last child graduating from high school)

I apologize for being so sentimental, but you've got to know that I'm the mom who cries at *Toy Story*! There should be a law against a mother having to go through so many changes all at once, but it doesn't work that way. These are the necessary seasons of our lives that will never return. I always knew the day would come when they would all be grown. I just didn't realize it would go so fast and take me by such surprise. Our lives are all so short. We only have a brief moment to love, nurture, and enjoy that precious childhood innocence. What a joy and a privilege to have been given this opportunity and all of the pleasures that it has to offer. I will be forever blessed that God has allowed me to live to watch my children grow up, and I am truly thankful. Now, I want to give so much back to the world and to all of those whose lives I touch.

My earnest prayer is that this book will touch countless lives, and that it will reach across barriers of all types of cancer—*all* illnesses, for that matter. I hope you will find new strength and the faith to face whatever you may be going through. Just know that you are never alone. I have a special place in my heart for all of you and care for you deeply. This is a common bond that we all share. May you feel the strength of my prayers for you.

Even after all of this time, my experience with cancer is still fresh in my mind, because I have been changed forever, and it has impacted my life in so many ways. Even so, I refuse to take ownership of cancer, and refuse to dwell on it any longer. Now, I would say that I control my own feelings and thoughts about cancer and they don't control me. Although I don't want any part of it, cancer has been a very real part of my life for quite some time. Now, I look at it as something necessary to bring me to where I am today, and that's as a much better person than I was in the beginning. I urge you to not linger too long on the past, but to look to the future with passion, hope, and anticipation. Each person's life is like an open book. It doesn't matter whether it's a short or a long story, but rather what does your story tell? Let your story shine in all its beauty, because no one else can tell it quite like you can.

No matter how hard we try to figure everything out, sometimes things will never make sense. I do know that God has a reason for everything. When we quit trying to figure everything out, we will eventually benefit from it later on. You have a choice to make, and you are the only one who can make it. When life gives you lemons, you can choose to become sour or you can add a little sugar and make lemonade

From my own experience, every new day is a gift. Life is so much sweeter. There's not enough time to dance, sing, and give hugs. Never withhold your love from others. Always tell them everyday how much you love them. Like you, I don't know what the future holds for me. The Bible says that the length of our days is uncertain, but I do know that I want to live every day to the fullest and love the most, laugh the hardest, and work and not complain. I never want to take a day or a person for granted. I want to make a difference in other people's lives around me so that when Jesus calls me home and looks into my eyes, I won't be ashamed. I want to feel like I've made a difference in even one person's life. I don't want to just go through the motions. I want to really feel it deep down in my spirit. I want to live one day at a time, placing everything in God's hands. If I can achieve all of that then I know that life is definitely worth *living*

Scripture:

For you shall go out with joy and be led forth with peace; the mountains and the hills shall break forth before you into singing, and all the trees of the field shall clap their hands.

Isaiah 55:12

Part Four

Helpful Resources

This final section of the book is mainly reference material for when you might need some extra help. Chapter Eighteen is written for the sole purpose of helping families and caregivers find somewhere to learn how to better relate to thyroid cancer patients. This may make the difference in making the best out of what is often an unbearable situation.

Chapter Nineteen is general information about thyroid cancer. I also list websites and cancer support groups for you to explore at your own convenience. Again, always check with your physician regarding your situation.

Chapter Twenty is the final chapter of the book and one of the most important. I've included as many uplifting Scriptures as I could find for you to read during those times when you feel that all hope is gone. During those times, the joy of the Lord will be your strength, and he will sustain you.

I hope that you find these last three chapters informative and helpful, and that any knowledge gained from reading them will be valuable to you. My earnest prayer is that it will bring healing to your body and your soul as well.

Chapter Eighteen

Special Words to Families and Caregivers of Thyroid Cancer Patients

This chapter is written to help those around you who may be as overwhelmed at your diagnosis as you are. Facing your diagnosis may be even more difficult for them because they are afraid to let you know how they feel. Like I've mentioned before, cancer affects everyone. It's a family thing. Talking about your feelings always helps to lighten the load. Keeping them bottled up will only make matters worse.

    I can't stress enough the importance of having someone to talk to when you are afraid and feel so alone, whether you are the patient or the caregiver. If you are a caregiver or a family member, let the patient cry on your shoulder, pray with and for them, and offer your help in any way that you can. But it's important for you to get proper rest and to take good care of yourself, also. Caregiving can drain you emotionally and physically, and you will need an outlet to avoid burning out. Try to get outside help for those days when you just can't cope. Don't feel selfish; you will be so much better for them when you take some time for yourself.

Sometimes the patient will just need to know that he or she is not alone. That is where your support will make a huge difference from day to day. Don't be alarmed when they get quiet and withdrawn. Even when they don't share with you everything they are feeling, they still need to know that they aren't alone. There will be days when they will want to talk and others when they seem to withdraw. Remember, this is a natural process they need to go through to absorb what is taking place in their life. They are trying to make some sense of it all.

If they've had surgery, they will need your assistance for a week or two, as it will take some time for them to regain their strength. They will particularly need help with meals. After surgery, the patient might not be hungry, but they still need healthy, nourishing meals in order to heal properly. Our church was wonderful, as they brought our family meals every day for several weeks. I'm not sure what we would have done without them. You might want to check with your church or someone else who would be willing to help with meals.

You might also help with household chores, and they will most certainly need help if they have small children or pets. Taking care of themselves after surgery is hard enough, without having the added stress of a family and pets to care for, too. After surgery, rest is so important to the healing process.

If the patient is preparing for the low-iodine diet, body scan, and possibly a radioactive iodine treatment, they will not be taking their thyroid medication. During that time, they will need quite a bit of help, because they will be extremely hypothyroid. Some of the symptoms of this might be mental fatigue, a slower heart rate, constipation, intolerance to cold and extreme tiredness, because the body processes are slowed down. This makes functioning very difficult. I couldn't even think properly. They will definitely not be themselves, and it will take some time once they are back on their medication before they will get back to their normal self again. While they are off their medication, the help they need could range anywhere from needing someone to talk to, to needing help in preparing the meals for their low-iodine diet. When you are extremely hypothyroid, cooking is the last thing you feel like doing.

If they require radiation and will be in isolation, they will need cards, phone calls, and any other way that communicates to them that you love them and are there for them to talk to when they are feeling sick or lonely.

Little kindnesses go a long way. You might surprise them with a bouquet of flowers or a balloon at their doorstep. They might like a good movie to help them avoid the lingering depression that is a very real part of the isolation.

It's so important to not pretend that everything is normal. Let them open up and talk about how they are feeling and talk to them about your feelings also. Keeping the lines of communication open during this difficult time is so important. Whatever you do, don't withdraw from the patient. If you do, this will send the message to them that they are all alone, which will cause them to retreat further into their own world. Try to be receptive to them.

You might need to drive them places when they are hypothyroid, because their reflexes will be slow. They will probably need to be taken to their doctor appointments.

Another task you might help with is to handle phone calls from well-meaning friends when they need to rest. Try to remain patient with them on those days when they are depressed or irritable. Put yourself in their place for a brief moment, and you will be more understanding of what they are going through.

It takes time to recuperate from surgery and radiation; several months to a year to regain their energy back, and sometimes longer. Time is the greatest healer.

Realize that your friend or loved one will probably come through this and will eventually be back to their old self again. You will have gained something along the way, which is a bond that cannot be broken. Your relationship will be strengthened because of your kindness and support at one of their weakest moments.

Scripture:
No one has greater love than to lay down his own life for his friends.

John 15:13

Chapter Nineteen

Facts and Resources about Thyroid Cancer

In this chapter, I give you as much information as I could find about thyroid cancer. Most of the information that I share with you is from my personal experience. I have also read numerous books and have explored many websites on the Internet. Once again, please follow your medical doctor's advice because each case is different. This is general knowledge that anyone can find with some research.

I am sure that by now you have tried to obtain as much information as possible. After I was diagnosed, that was something I did. Like a sponge, I took in everything that I could to learn as much as possible in order to cope with such a diagnosis. I would have grasped at anything if it would have been beneficial in curing cancer. When you are feeling that desperate, every bit of knowledge is precious. This chapter is a tool to aid you in your search to find out everything that you can and to feel like you are taking a proactive approach. Being informed about your type of cancer and the latest treatment options available to you can help ease your mind. At the same time, you can be bombarded with too much information for your own good. This can be as confusing as not having enough. In the past, people lacked the proper resources, but today we have a wealth of information at our fingertips.

Your doctor is extremely important, but he or she can only do so much. Once they've done their part, it's up to you to do everything you can possibly do yourself, to combat this disease.

No one likes the C word. Just a few years ago, thyroid cancer would have probably been terminal, but new research has saved many lives, and they are constantly looking for a cure. But even with tremendous progress in research, cancer is still an enemy to be feared. Millions of Americans and people all over the world are under medical care for some type of cancer. Early detection and breakthroughs in treatment are key factors in beating this dreaded disease.

Despite the type of cancer, all have one similarity: normal cells have gone wild.

In this journey where much patience is learned, I am so thankful that thyroid cancer is usually a very treatable form of cancer and, in most cases, can be cured.

We need to understand how our bodies work in the first place. Before we were diagnosed, we should have been taking good care of ourselves. Like I explained in chapter fourteen, we can't blame ourselves or anyone else for our cancer diagnosis. Sometimes nothing we could have done previously would have prevented cancer, but its common sense to take responsibility for our own health and to stay as fit and healthy as we can. We owe it to ourselves and our loved ones. I believe prevention is very important.

In this chapter, I will be answering many of your questions:

1. What is the thyroid, and how does it affect the body?
2. How is Thyroid Cancer diagnosed and what are the symptoms?
3. How do I cope with the diagnosis?
4. What are my treatment options?
5. What are the risk factors?
6. How is thyroid cancer staged?
7. What is the chance of a recurrence?
8. What happens after the treatment?
9. What are the benefits of thyroid cancer support groups?
10. Websites and additional resources

1. What is the thyroid and how does it affect the body?

The thyroid is a gland in the neck. It has two kinds of cells that make hormones. Follicular cells make thyroid hormone, which affect heart rate, body temperature, and energy level. C cells make calcitonin, a hormone that helps control the level of calcium in the blood.

The thyroid is shaped like a butterfly. It lies in the front of the neck, beneath your voice box, (larynx). It has two lobes, which are separated by a thin section called the isthmus. A healthy thyroid is a little larger than a quarter, weighing less than one ounce. It's amazing how such a small part of the body can cause so much trouble, when it's not working properly.

A swollen lobe might look or feel like a lump in the front of the neck. A swollen thyroid is called a goiter. Most goiters are caused by a lack of iodine in the diet. Iodine is found in shellfish and iodized salt. The follicular cells use iodine from the blood to make thyroid hormone and help to regulate metabolism. Every cell in the body depends upon Thyroid metabolism. Too much thyroid hormone is a condition called hyperthyroidism. It can cause a rapid or irregular heartbeat, trouble sleeping, nervousness, hunger, weight loss, and a feeling of being too warm. Too little hormone, known as hypothyroidism, can cause a person to slow down, feel tired, and gain weight. The amount of thyroid hormone released by the thyroid is regulated by the pituitary gland, which makes a substance called thyroid stimulating hormone, or TSH. It's no wonder I felt like Dr. Jekyll and Mr. Hyde sometimes, because I dangled between both extremes at times. That's what I mean by having the correct dose of medication regulated.

Many people have thyroid problems, without having cancer. There are common tests to examine Thyroid Gland function. No one single laboratory test is 100% accurate in diagnosing all types of thyroid disease, however, a combination of two or more tests can usually detect even the slightest abnormality of thyroid function.

2. **How is Thyroid Cancer diagnosed, and what are the symptoms?**

All cancers begin in cells, the body's basic unit of life. Cells make up tissues and tissues make up the organs of the body. Normally, cells grow and divide to form new cells as the body needs them. When cells grow old and die, new cells take their place. Sometimes, this orderly process goes wrong. New cells form when the body does not need them, and old cells do not die when they should. These extra cells can form a mass of tissue called a growth or tumor. Growths on the thyroid are usually called nodules. Many types of tumors can develop in the thyroid gland. Many of them are benign or non cancerous, about 90%, but others are malignant or cancerous. This means they can spread into nearby tissues and throughout the body. There are many reasons the thyroid gland might be larger than usual, and it's usually not cancer. When hormones get out of balance, it can cause a goiter. Lumps in the thyroid gland are called thyroid nodules. Most thyroid nodules are benign. About 1 in 20 is cancerous. Thyroid nodules can develop at any age, but it's more common in older adults. Most nodules are cysts filled with fluid. Solid nodules have little fluid. Benign thyroid nodules can, sometimes, be left untreated as long as they're not growing or causing symptoms. Different cancers develop from each kind of cell. The differences are important because they affect how serious the cancer is and what type of treatment is needed. Malignant nodules are cancer. They are generally more serious and may sometimes be life threatening. Thyroid cancer is the most common endocrine cancer. It occurs in all age groups from children through seniors. There are several types of thyroid cancer; papillary, follicular, medullary, anaplastic, and variants.

Papillary and follicular carcinomas are referred to as well differentiated thyroid cancer and account tor 80-90% of all thyroid cancers. Variants include tall cell, insular, columnar, and Hurthle cell. Their treatment and management are similar. If detected early, most papillary and follicular thyroid cancer can be treated successfully.

Medullary thyroid carcinoma accounts for 5-10% of all thyroid cancers. Medullary cancer is easier to treat and control if found before it spreads to other parts of the body.
Anaplastic thyroid carcinoma is the least common and accounts for only 1-2% of all thyroid cancer. This type is difficult to control

and treat because it is a very aggressive type of thyroid cancer. The cancer cells tend to grow and spread very quickly.

If thyroid cancer spreads (metastasizes) outside the thyroid, cancer cells are often found in nearby lymph nodes, nerves, or blood vessels. If the cancer has reached these lymph nodes, cancer cells may also have spread to other lymph nodes or to other organs, such as the lungs or bones. When cancer spreads from its original place to another part of the body, the new tumor has the same name as the primary tumor. For example, if thyroid cancer spreads to the lungs, the cancer cells in the lungs are thyroid cancer cells. The disease is metastatic thyroid cancer, not lung cancer. It is treated as thyroid cancer, not as lung cancer. Doctors sometimes call the new tumor "distant" or metastatic disease.

In 2010, 44,670 new cases of Thyroid Cancer were diagnosed. There were 1,690 deaths in 2010 from Thyroid Cancer

Symptoms:

Early thyroid cancer often does not cause symptoms. But as the cancer grows, symptoms may include:

- A lump, or nodule, in the front of the neck near the Adam's apple;
- Hoarseness or difficulty speaking in a normal voice;
- Swollen lymph nodes, especially in the neck;
- Difficulty swallowing or breathing; or
- Pain in the throat or neck.

These symptoms are not sure signs of thyroid cancer. An infection, a benign goiter, or another problem could also cause these symptoms. Anyone with these symptoms should see a doctor as soon as possible. Only a doctor can diagnose and treat the problem.

If a person has symptoms that suggest thyroid cancer, the doctor may perform a physical exam and ask about the patient's personal and family medical history. The doctor may also order laboratory tests and imaging tests to produce pictures of the Thyroid and other areas.

The exams and tests may include the following:

- Physical exam—The doctor will feel the neck, thyroid, voice box, and lymph nodes in the neck for unusual growths (nodules) or swelling.
- Blood tests—The doctor may test for abnormal levels (too low or too high) of thyroid-stimulating hormone (TSH) in the blood. TSH is made by the pituitary gland in the brain. It stimulates the release of thyroid hormone.
- Ultrasonography—The ultrasound device uses sound waves that people cannot hear. The waves bounce off the thyroid, and a computer uses the echoes to create a picture called a sonogram. From the picture, the doctor can see how many nodules are present, how big they are, and whether they are solid or filled with fluid
- Radionuclide scanning—The doctor may order a nuclear medicine scan that uses a very small amount of radioactive material to make thyroid nodules show up on a picture. Nodules that absorb less radioactive material than the surrounding thyroid tissue are called cold nodules. Cold nodules may be benign or malignant. Hot nodules take up

more radioactive material than surrounding thyroid tissue and are usually benign.
- Biopsy—The removal of tissue to look for cancer cells is called a biopsy. A biopsy can show cancer, tissue changes that may lead to cancer, and other conditions. A biopsy is the only sure way to know whether a nodule is cancerous. The doctor may remove tissue through a needle or during surgery.
- Fine needle aspiration—For most patients, the doctor removes a sample of tissue from a thyroid nodule with a thin needle. A pathologist looks at the cells under a microscope to look for cancer. Sometimes, the doctor uses an ultrasound device to guide the needle through the nodule.
- Surgical biopsy—If a diagnosis cannot be made from the fine-needle aspiration, the doctor may operate to remove the nodule. A pathologist then checks the tissues for cancer cells.

3. **How do I cope with the diagnosis?**

This can be the hardest part after taking in so much information all at once. This is a very frightening time for you. You will have many questions and may feel overwhelmed. Write down all of your concerns and talk to your doctor about them. You will probably have many different emotions, such as shock, panic, fear, anger, denial, and, eventually, acceptance. Everyone handles their diagnosis differently. Some people may not have all of these emotions. It varies from person to person.

In most cases, thyroid cancer is one of the most treatable kinds of cancer, but you will still have to be treated for it. There's no way around it. There are many tests and doctor visits that you will have to endure, especially the first year. Keep your focus on getting better. Don't lose hope. I'm here to encourage you and to tell you that you can do it! Yes, you can!

4. What are my treatment options and side effects of treatments?

After Thyroid Cancer is found, your doctor will discuss treatment options with you. In choosing a treatment plan, factors to consider include the type and stage of the cancer, and your general health. People with thyroid cancer often want to take an active part in making decisions about their medical care. They want to learn all they can about their disease and their treatment choices. Sometimes the shock they are going through at first after being diagnosed with cancer makes it hard for them to think of everything they need to ask the doctor. It helps to make a list of questions to ask the doctor before an appointment. Sometimes it helps to take a family member or a friend to your appointments with you. The doctor may refer patients to doctors (oncologists) who specialize in treating cancer. Specialists who treat thyroid cancer include surgeons, endocrinologists, and radiation oncologists. Treatment usually begins within a few weeks after the diagnosis. Before starting treatment, the patient might want a second opinion about the diagnosis and the treatment plan. The doctor and patient can work together to develop a treatment plan that is right for the patient. Treatment depends on a number of factors, including the type of thyroid cancer, the size of the nodule, the patient's age, and whether the cancer has spread. Surgery is the most common treatment for thyroid cancer. The surgeon may remove all or part of the thyroid.

The type of surgery depends on the type and stage of thyroid cancer, the size of the nodule and the patient's age. A total thyroidectomy is surgery to remove the entire thyroid gland. The surgeon removes the thyroid through an incision in the neck. Nearby lymph nodes are sometimes removed. If the pathologist finds cancer cells in the lymph nodes, it means that the disease could spread to other parts of the body. Patients are often uncomfortable for the first few days after surgery. However, medicine can usually control their pain. It is also common for patients to feel tired and weak. The length of time it takes to recover from an operation varies for each patient. After surgery to remove the thyroid and nearby tissues or organs, such as the parathyroid glands, patients may need to take medicine (thyroid hormone) or vitamin and mineral supplements (vitamin D and calcium) to replace the lost functions of these organs. In a few cases, certain nerves or muscles may be damaged or removed during surgery. If this happens, the patient may have voice problems. Some patients who have a total thyroidectomy also receive radioactive iodine or external radiation therapy. Some patients with papillary or follicular cancer may be treated with lobotomy. The lobe with the cancerous nodule is removed. Nearly all patients who have part or the entire thyroid removed will take thyroid hormone pills to replace the natural hormone. Radioactive iodine therapy uses radioactive iodine (I-131) to destroy thyroid cancer cells anywhere in the body. The therapy is usually given by mouth (liquid or capsules). The intestine absorbs the I-131, which flows through the bloodstream and collects in thyroid cells. Thyroid cancer cells remaining in the neck and those that have spread to other parts of the body are killed when they absorb I-131. Within three weeks, only traces of radioactive iodine remain in the body. Some patients have nausea and vomiting on the first day of

I-131therapy. Thyroid tissue remaining in the neck after surgery may become swollen and painful. If the thyroid cancer has spread to other parts of the body, the I-131 that collects there may cause pain and swelling. Patients may also have a dry mouth or lose their sense of taste or smell for a short time after I-131 therapy. Chewing sugar free gum or sucking on sugar free hard candy may help. During treatment, patients are encouraged to drink lots of water and other fluids because fluids help I-131 pass out of the body more quickly. Researchers have reported that a very small number of patients may develop Leukemia years after treatment with high doses of I-131. Hormone treatment after surgery is usually part of the treatment plan for papillary and follicular cancer. When a patient takes thyroid hormone pills, the growth of any remaining thyroid cancer cells slows down; this lowers the chance that the disease will return. Thyroid hormone pills seldom cause side effects, but a few patients may get a rash or lose some of their hair during the first few months of treatment. The doctor will closely monitor the level of thyroid hormone in the blood during follow up visits. Too much thyroid hormone may cause patients to lose weight and to feel hot and sweaty. It may also cause chest pain, cramps, and diarrhea. This condition is called, hyperthyroidism. If the thyroid level is too low, the patient may gain weight, feel cold and have dry skin and hair. This condition is called hypothyroidism. If necessary, the doctor will adjust the dose so that the patient takes the right amount. External radiation therapy uses high energy rays to kill cancer cells. A large machine directs radiation at the neck or at parts of the body where the cancer has spread. It affects cancer cells only in the treated area. External radiation therapy is used mainly to treat people with advanced thyroid cancer that does not respond to radioactive iodine therapy. External radiation therapy may cause patients to become very tired as treatment continues. Resting is important, but doctors usually advise patients to try to stay as active as they can. In addition, when patients receive external radiation therapy, it is common for their skin to become red, dry, and tender in the treated area. When the neck is treated, patients may feel hoarse or have trouble swallowing. Another treatment option for thyroid cancer is Chemotherapy. This is the use of drugs that will kill cancer cells. These drugs enter the bloodstream and travel throughout the body. For some patients, chemotherapy may be combined with external radiation therapy. The side effects of chemotherapy depend mainly on the specific drugs that are used. The most common side effects include nausea and vomiting, mouth sores, loss of appetite and hair loss. Some of these side effects may be relieved with medicine. Because cancer treatment may damage healthy cells and tissues, unwanted side effects sometimes occur. These side effects depend on many factors, including the type and extent of the treatment. They may not be the same for each person. The health care team may suggest ways to help the patient manage them.

Radioactive Iodine (RAI)

The following information may seem a bit lengthy, but it is a detailed summary about the Radioactive Iodine treatment and low iodine diet. If you have had thyroid cancer, it may be likely that you will need this treatment, depending on your doctor's opinion. I feel that this information will be beneficial to you at this time. This information is obtained by permission from THYCA, Thyroid Cancer association. If you go to their website, you can download the free Low-Iodine Cookbook.

The Low-Iodine Diet

Thyroid cancer patients with papillary or follicular thyroid cancer often receive a dose of radioactive iodine (RAI) about two months after their surgery in an attempt to destroy (ablate) any remaining thyroid cells in their bodies.

Most of these thyroid cancer patients also undergo whole-body radiation scans at periodic intervals, using a "tracer" dose of RAI. If their scan is not "clean," they may then receive treatment with a larger dose of RAI in an attempt to eliminate remaining thyroid cells.

In preparation for an RAI scan or RAI treatment, patients are usually asked to go on a low-iodine diet (LID). The diet is to prepare for the RAI. The patient follows the diet when preparing for RAI either by temporarily stopping levothyroxine (withdrawal) or be receiving injections of Thyrogen (recombinant TSH) while continuing on levothyroxine.

The purpose of a low-iodine diet is to deplete the body of its stores of iodine, to help increase the effectiveness of the radioactive iodine scan or treatment. The premise is that when the radioactive iodine is administered, the thyroid cells will "suck" up the iodine, because the body has been so depleted.

This diet is for a short time period. The usual time period is around two weeks (14 days) or slightly more. The diet usually begins around two weeks before the testing and treatment period, but it can vary, depending on the patient's individual case.

The following is a combination of diet guidelines from several ThyCa medical advisors. Your physician may have different guidelines. Please check with your doctor before you start the diet.

General Comments

- Remember: LOW IODINE has NOTHING TO DO WITH SODIUM. The diet is a low-iodine diet, NOT a low-sodium diet. Sodium is in most foods. Table salt is sodium chloride, not sodium.
- Sodium in any form is OK, as long as it is not provided as IODIZED salt. NON-IODIZED salt is OK for the diet, as long as it is not sea salt. As noted below, you should avoid any product or ingredient from the sea, because sea based products are high in iodine.
- Also, this is a "low-iodine diet, NOT a "no-iodine" and NOT an 'iodine-free" diet.
- During your time on the diet, you may freely eat any foods that are low in iodine. There are lots of foods that you can eat.
- For recipes and a snack list, use ThyCa's free Low Iodine Cookbook. You can download it free from their website and print it out.
- You can also adapt your favorite recipes from your own cookbooks to the low-iodine diet, by eliminating ingredients that are high in iodine.

Avoid These Foods and Additives

Avoid the following foods, starting when instructed by your physician before your radioactive iodine test or treatment. Continue as instructed after your radioactive iodine treatment (often for about 24 hours after). These foods are high in iodine.

- Iodized salt and sea salt and any foods containing iodized salt or sea salt. Non-iodized salt may be used. For example,

Kosher salt is okay unless the label says that it is iodized or sea salt.
- Seafood and sea products (fish, shellfish, seaweed, seaweed tablets, kelp). These are all very high in iodine and should be avoided.
- Dairy products (milk, cheese, cream, yogurt, butter, ice cream, powdered dairy creamers, whey, casein, other dairy products.
- Egg yolks or whole eggs or foods containing whole eggs. Egg whites are acceptable, because they contain little or no iodine.
- Commercial bakery products. Avoid bread products that contain iodine/iodate dough conditioners (usually small bakery breads are alright; it's best to bake it yourself or substitute with Matzos).
- Red Dye #3. ThyCa suggests that you avoid red, orange or brown processed foods, pills and capsules.
- Most Chocolate (for its milk content). Cocoa powder and some dark chocolates are permitted. The ThyCa cookbook has recipes for permitted chocolate.
- Some Molasses. Avoid if sulfured or blackstrap. It's okay to use the milder, fairly sweet unsulfured molasses usually used in cooking and that is the type most often available in grocery stores.
- Soybeans and most soy products (soy sauce, soy milk, and tofu). Soy oil and soy lecithin are both okay.
- Some beans besides soybeans, including red kidney beans, lima beans, navy beans, pinto beans and cowpeas.
- Some diets say to avoid rhubarb and potato skins, but the inside of the potato is fine.

- Iodine-containing vitamins and Food Supplements. Most vitamins with minerals contain iodine.
- If you are taking a medication that contains iodine, check with your physician.

Limit the amounts of these Foods

Some diets from thyroid cancer specialists recommend limiting the daily intake of foods that are moderate in iodine: 5 to 20 mcg per serving.

- Fresh meats. Up to 5 ounces per day of fresh meats such as chicken, beef, pork, lamb and veal are fine on the low-iodine diet. Whole cuts tend to contain less iodine than do ground meats. Also, check the package label on meats, including whole turkeys, turkey breasts, turkey cutlets, chicken and all pork products.
- Grains, cereals. Up to 4 servings per day of grains, cereals, pasta, and breads without iodine-containing ingredients are fine on this diet.
- Rices, because they vary in the amount of iodine depending on the region where they are grown, so rice should be eaten only in limited amounts. Some low-iodine diets recommend avoiding rice.

What about Restaurant Foods and Fast Food?

Although restaurants generally use non-iodized salt, it is not possible to know whether a particular restaurant is using iodized salt or sea salt. The ingredients that chain and fast-food restaurants use may change. ThyCa suggests that you avoid restaurant foods other than plain juices or soft drinks, or the inside of a plain baked potato.

What About Manufactured and Processed Foods?

If fresh foods are available, many patients prefer to eat fresh foods during the short period of being on the low-iodine diet. They avoid processed food, because it is not known for sure whether or not iodized salt has been used. For any processed food, it is also important to read the label to be sure there is no Red Dye #3.

Read the ingredient labels on all packaged foods and spices.

Foods That Are Fine to Eat on the Low-Iodine Diet

The low-iodine diet consists mostly of fresh, low-fat, low-calorie foods. Because of this, following this diet greatly reduces the tendency to gain weight while hypothyroid.

The following foods and ingredients are fine to eat. You do not need to limit the quantity, except as noted.

- **Fresh fruits and fruit juices, except rhubarb, maraschino cherries (if they contain Red Dye #3), and fruit cocktail with maraschino cherries.**
- **Vegetables, preferably raw and fresh-cooked or frozen without salt.**
- **Unsalted nuts and unsalted nut butters.**
- **Grain/cereal products in moderate amounts.**
- **Fresh chicken, beef, and other meats in moderate amounts**

- Sugar, jelly, honey, maple syrup, and unsulfured molasses.
- Black pepper and fresh or dried herbs.
- All vegetable oils. Salad dressings provided they contain only allowed ingredients.
- Homemade foods (see the free Low-Iodine Cookbook from the ThyCa website.
- Cola, diet cola, lemonade, sodas (except with Red Dye #3) non-instant coffee and tea

Food prepared from fresh meats, fresh poultry, fresh or frozen vegetables, and fresh fruits should be fine for this diet, provided that you do not add any of the iodine-containing ingredients listed above. The cookbook also has a handy snack list.

A Final Note

The key to coping well with this diet is being prepared ahead of time, especially if you are preparing for RAI by stopping your levothyroxine pills and becoming hypothyroid. Before you start becoming hypothyroid, prepare the basics and freeze. It will make it so much easier. For the snack list, ThyCa suggests that you stock up on snack items from the list for times when you do not feel like cooking. and that you use the cookbook like thousands of other thyroid cancer survivors have used.

After Receiving Radioactive Iodine

After receiving RAI for a scan, you will go home immediately. After your RAI treatment dose, you may be sent home immediately, or you may stay in the hospital for one or more days. Your home circumstances, such as whether there is an infant at home, may affect the decision about going home or staying at the hospital after your treatment.

If You Go Home Immediately After Receiving RAI

Radioactive iodine decreases the function of thyroid cells and inhibits their ability to grow. It is given in liquid or pill form and goes directly to the thyroid gland where it is absorbed by the thyroid tissue. Most of the radioactive iodine will be received by your thyroid gland. Any radioactive iodine not collected by the thyroid gland will be eliminated during the first few days through urine, feces, saliva and sweat. The following steps listed below will help assure that the excreted radiation from your body does not contaminate the environment or cause harm to other people.

What do I do at home?

If you go home immediately after a treatment dose, use the following guidelines regarding distance, time, and hygiene.

- Minimize contact with everyone for the first five days and with small children or pregnant women for eight days.
- Do not sit next to someone in an automobile for more than one hour.
- Sleep in a separate room and use separate bath linen and launder these and underclothing separately for one week.
- Wash your hands with soap and plenty of water every time you use the toilet.
- Rinse the sink and tub thoroughly after using them.

- Use separate eating utensils or disposable eating utensils. Wash eating utensils separately for one week. Do not prepare food for others.
- Flush toilet 2-3 times after use for two weeks after discharge.
- Discuss with your doctor how long you should wait before starting a pregnancy after your treatment.
- If you are breastfeeding, it should be discontinued.

Information during your Hospital Stay

After the doctor has given you your treatment you are to remain in your room with the door closed until you are released from isolation by the radiation safety officer. This is usually one or more days. This can be a great time to get caught up on things such as reading magazines or talking to friends and family on the telephone. It is strongly advised that there be no visitors. If you do have visitors, a maximum of 30 minutes is allowed only. Visitors must wear gloves, protective shoe covers and a gown before entering the room. Pregnant women and children under the age of 18 may not visit during your hospital stay. Although, your nurse will spend very little time in your room, you can communicate frequently with your nurse by using the telephone. You will have to wear a hospital gown during your hospital stay and hospital slippers to avoid contamination of your own clothes by perspiration. Your mattress and pillow will be covered with plastic. You will need to dispose all linen and garbage in plastic bags provided in your room. All cutlery and dishes are to be disposed in a plastic bag. You will remain on a low-iodine diet.

General Information:

Showering two or three times a day and washing your hair will help remove the excreted radiation through perspiration. Sucking on sour candies for the first 24-48 hours after radioiodine therapy is recommended by thyroid cancer specialists to help reduce excessive radiation to your salivary glands.

Radioactive Iodine Treatment—Side Effects

- Sore Throat/Hoarseness. Salivary glands affected by RAI treatment may become swollen.
- Vomiting
- Headache. Tylenol can be used
- Constipation/Diarrhea.
- Fatigue. Resting is good

Signs to Watch in Case of Drug Reaction

- Shortness of breath
- Chills
- Fever
- Rash

External Beam Radiation Therapy

External beam radiation is sometimes given as a treatment in addition to the primary treatment, or as a curative treatment when the cancer cannot be removed by surgery, or as a palliative approach to relieve symptoms and improve quality of life.

External beam radiation therapy involves a series of daily outpatient treatments to accurately deliver radiation to the cancer. It is important to take care of your mouth, teeth and gums during radiation. Careful brushing of your teeth can help prevent tooth decay, gum disease, mouth sores and infections. Be sure to tell your dentist that you received radiation to the head and neck area.

5. What are the risk factors?

Risk factors associated with thyroid cancer include a family history of thyroid cancer, gender (women have a higher incidence of thyroid cancer), age (the majority of cases occur in people over 40, although thyroid cancer affects all age groups from children through seniors), and prior exposure of the thyroid gland to radiation.

6. How is Thyroid Cancer staged?

Staging is the process of finding out how far a cancer has spread. The stage of a cancer is one of the most important factors in choosing treatment options and predicting your chance for cure and long term survival. Staging is based on the results of the physical exam, biopsy, and imaging tests, such as, ultrasound, CT scan, MRI, chest x-ray, and nuclear medicine scans. Staging is a standard way for the cancer care team to summarize how large a cancer is, and how far it has spread.

7 What is the chance of a recurrence?

While the prognosis for most thyroid cancer patients is very good, the rate of recurrence can be up to 30%, and recurrences can occur even decades after the initial diagnosis. Therefore, it is important that patients get regular follow-up examinations to detect whether the cancer has re-emerged. Monitoring should continue throughout the patient's lifetime. Periodic follow-up examinations can include a review of the medical history together with selected blood tests appropriate for the type of cancer and stage of treatment, physical examination, and imaging techniques (ultrasound, radioiodine whole body scan, chest X-ray, CT, MRI, PET, and other tests).

8. What happens after the treatment?

Follow up care after treatment for Thyroid Cancer is an important part of the overall treatment plan. Regular checkups make sure that any changes in health are caught early, so that any problems can be found and treated as soon as possible. The doctor will explain a follow up plan, and let the patient know how often to schedule appointments. Thanks to new improved therapies, an increasing number of people are living beyond cancer and enjoying a full life after treatment. Staying healthy can be a challenge for cancer survivors, because treatments create long lasting health needs for the duration of the patient's life. As with any cancer treatment, there can be side effects from certain treatment, but most people do very well after treatment. Follow up care is very important, because thyroid cancers grow slowly and can recur even 10 to 20 years after initial treatment. Lifestyle changes are so important for cancer survivors. Making healthier choices are important. Diet and nutrition play an important role in the healing process. Some of the things a cancer survivor should do are as follows:

- Eat five or more servings of vegetables and fruit each day.
- Choose whole grain foods instead of white flour and sugars.
- Limit meats high in fat.
- Cut back on processed meats, like hot dogs, bologna, and bacon.
- Limit alcohol consumption.
- Get regular exercise.

This combination will help you maintain a healthy weight, and keep you feeling more energetic. Rest is also important in regaining your strength after treatment. Fatigue is a very common symptom in people being treated for cancer. Exercise can help reduce fatigue. It's easy to become depressed during this fatigue, from feeling so tired. Talk to your health care provider before any exercise programs, but starting out with short walks may be beneficial. Depending on how tired you are, you may need to balance activity with periods of rest. Exercise can improve your physical and emotional health.

- It improves your heart and circulation.
- It strengthens your muscles.
- It reduces fatigue.
- It lowers anxiety and depression.
- It makes you feel happier.
- It helps you feel better about yourself.
- Long term, we know that exercise plays a role in preventing some cancers.

9. What are the benefits of cancer support groups?

At such a difficult time, it's almost a necessity to find some type of a support group. Your family and friends can and should be the first place to start. It's also very helpful to talk to others who are going through the same thing that you are, or have been through it previously. A Thyroid Cancer diagnosis is frightening. You will have a lot of questions and concerns. You may want to learn more about Thyroid Cancer or just simply need to talk to someone else about your fears. It's so important to be able to vent, laugh, cry, or to just be understood, especially by someone else who has been through the same thing you are going through. As much as your family and friends care, they really can't quite comprehend all of the issues you are facing, unless they have gone through it themselves. It's important to be able to share some of your feelings with someone else who can relate on the same level, to what you are dealing with, and who have walked in your shoes. The emotional support that you will gain is crucial during this time in your life. There are many people to talk to and many resources available to patients and families. There are also many types of counseling available. Also, online support groups can provide advice and support, as well. They can offer strength and comfort. Some of the following support groups can be from family, friends, and community organized cancer support groups, church groups or online support. The much needed emotional strength a cancer patient can benefit from, is also a step in the right direction towards a quicker recovery.

Connecting with others who are going through the same form of Thyroid Cancer is very helpful. The patient can ask questions and get answers from others who are also dealing with the disease. This helps the patient feel that they aren't alone. Support groups can help after the diagnosis, during treatment, and beyond, as the patient is coming to terms with how his or her life will be changed, even for many years to come, beyond the final treatment. Some people enjoy a group setting, while others like to remain anonymous, or to have individual counseling. What's best for you depends on your situation and personality. Some people just like to stay at home and talk from their computer, while others need a hug, or a pat on the back. No matter which avenue you take, it can be a lonely journey, so don't go it all alone.

10. **Websites and additional resources:**

Listed below are some websites and resources to refer to for additional help. You can find many more of them if you do some research and explore various websites. You can also read good books. Ask your doctor. He or she is the best place to start.

1. **ThyCa: Thyroid Cancer Survivors' Association Inc. (This is where I have obtained most of the information for this book. I have only touched base with the most important topics. For a more thorough explanation, please go to their website or call them).**

    P.O. Box 1545
    New York, NY 10159-1545
    Phone: 877-588-7904
    Fax: 630-604-6078

    ThyCa is a National nonprofit organization developing programs to link survivors and health care professionals around the world. Their website maintains current information about Thyroid Cancer, and support services available to people at any stage of testing, treatment or lifelong monitoring for Thyroid Cancer, as well as their caregivers. It receives ongoing input and review from numerous Thyroid Cancer specialists. The site also serves as a resource for anyone interested in Thyroid Cancer survivors' issues, and includes news for survivors about online chats, conferences, mailing lists, and local support groups. ThyCa is a sponsor of Thyroid Cancer Awareness Month. September is Thyroid Cancer Awareness Month.

ThyCa contains facts about all types of thyroid cancer and their treatments. They have been in operation since 1995.

National Cancer Institute
www.cancer.gov
800-4-CANCER

American Cancer Society
www.cancer.org
800-227-2345

Cancer Treatment Centers of America
www.cancercenter.com
866-952-4223

2. **My email address:**

classymom06@yahoo.com

I would be happy to encourage anyone who needs someone to talk to and pray with.

In Summary:

Once you're out of treatment and life calms down a bit, you may wonder, "What am I supposed to do now?" Developing a survivorship plan is an important step in being proactive about your health care needs. This means knowing what symptoms to look for that might signify a recurrence. Following a good diet and exercise plan is crucial to your overall health. This is why it can't be stressed enough to keep all of your follow-up appointments. Doctors are constantly looking for new advances and more effective approaches for treating thyroid cancer. Stay informed, get the word out, and encourage others who may be undergoing some of the same things that you have. By all means, get involved! Find out all that you possibly can. Maybe when you're feeling up to it, you could run a marathon or volunteer for the American Cancer Society. Keep fighting! Don't let your candle be snuffed out, but keep the flame alive by doing all that you can for your own life and for all those people who are following behind you!

This leaves us with the final question, one that I regretfully need to address:

What do you do if treatment is no longer working?

If it seems that a cure is not possible, the goal may be to remove or destroy as much of the cancer as possible, to prevent the tumor from growing, spreading, or returning for as long as possible. If you have any concerns, sometimes it is better to get a second opinion.

Whatever you decide, it is important to be made as comfortable as possible. You may benefit from hospice care at some point.

Maintaining hope is important. This should be an important time to refocus on the most important things in your life. You can still hope for good times with family and friends, times that are filled with as much happiness as you can find.

I want to leave you with one final thought. Never lose your focus on the awesome presence of the Lord. He will never leave your side. His love for you will carry you *through* any storm! I love you, my friend!

Scripture:

For the Lamb Who is in the midst of the throne will be their Shepherd, and he will guide them to the springs of the waters of life; and God will wipe away every tear from their eyes.

Revelation 7:17

God will wipe away every tear from their eyes; and death shall be no more, neither shall there be anguish (sorrow or mourning) nor grief nor pain any more, for the old conditions and the former order of things have passed away.

Revelation 21:4

They shall see his face, and His name shall be on their foreheads. And there shall be no more night; they have no need for lamplight or sunlight, for the Lord God will illuminate them and be their light, and they shall reign forever and ever.

Revelation 22:4-5

Chapter Twenty

Uplifting Scriptures

In this chapter, I have included as many uplifting Scriptures as I could find to lift your spirits while you are going through this entire process. It's important to meditate on them as often as you can until they calm your spirit with God's peace and healing. As you let these Scriptures sink in, they will increase your faith and give you the strength you need from day to day. Keep claiming these wonderful healing Scriptures, and eventually you will notice a difference. You'll not only start feeling better physically, but emotionally and spiritually as well.

I pray that God's blessings will be upon you and that you will be given an adequate supply of strength to face each new day, as only he can do.

All of these scriptures are taken from the Amplified Bible.

- **Psalm 46:1-2** God is our Refuge and Strength, a very present and well-proved help in trouble. Therefore we will not fear,

though the earth should change and though the mountains be shaken into the midst of the seas.
- **Psalm 46:10** Let be and be still, and know that I am God. I will be exalted among the nations! I will be exalted in the earth!
- **Jeremiah 29:11** For I know the thoughts and plans that I have for you, says the Lord, thoughts and plans for welfare and peace and not for evil, to give you hope in your final outcome.
- **1 Thessalonians 5:11** Therefore encourage one another and edify one another, just as you are doing.
- **Matthew 10:30** But even the very hairs of your head are numbered.
- **John 3:16** For God so greatly loved and dearly prized the world that he gave up his only begotten Son, so that whoever believes in Him shall not perish, but have eternal life.
- **Zephaniah 3:17** The Lord your God is in the midst of you, a Mighty One, a Savior. He will rejoice over you with joy; He will rest and in His love He will be silent and make no mention of past sins, or even recall them; He will exult over you with singing.
- **Colossians 1:11** That you may be invigorated and strengthened with all power according to the might of his glory, every kind of endurance and patience with joy.
- **Nehemiah 8:10** Go your way, eat the fat, drink the sweet drink, and send portions to him for whom nothing is prepared; for this day is holy to our Lord. And be not grieved and depressed, for the joy of the Lord is your strength and stronghold.
- **Proverbs 15:13** A glad heart makes a cheerful countenance, but by sorrow of heart the spirit is broken.

- **Proverbs 20:24** Man's steps are ordered by the Lord. How then can a man understand his way?
- **Proverbs 3:5** Lean on, trust in, and be confident in the Lord with all your heart and mind and do not rely on your own insight or understanding.
- **2 Corinthians 12:9** But he said to me, My grace is enough for you; for my strength and power are made perfect and show themselves most effective in your weakness. Therefore, I will all the more gladly glory in my weaknesses and infirmities, that the strength and power of Christ may rest upon me!
- **Hebrews 11:1** Now faith is the assurance of the things we hope for, being the proof of things we do not see and the conviction of their reality.
- **Proverbs 18:14** The strong spirit of a man sustains him in bodily pain or trouble, but a weak and broken spirit who can raise up or bear?
- **Proverbs 18:21** Death and life are in the power of the tongue, and they who indulge in it shall eat the fruit of it for death or life.
- **Matthew 5:4** Blessed and enviably happy are those who mourn, for they shall be comforted!
- **Jonah 2:2** I cried out of my distress to the Lord, and he heard me;
- **2 Corinthians 1:3-4** Blessed be the God and Father of our Lord Jesus Christ, the Father of sympathy and the God of every comfort, Who comforts us in every trouble, so that we also may be able to comfort those who are in any kind of trouble or distress, with the comfort with which we ourselves are comforted by God.

- **Exodus 33:14** And the Lord said, My Presence shall go with you, and I will give you rest
- **Job 19:25-27** For I know that my Redeemer and Vindicator lives, and at last he will stand upon the earth. And after my skin, even this body, has been destroyed, then from my flesh or without it I shall see God, whom I, even I, shall see for myself and on my side! And my eyes shall behold Him, and not as a stranger! My heart pines away and is consumed within me.
- **Psalm 18:29** For by You I can run through a troop, and by my God I can leap over a wall.
- **Psalm 34:18-19** The Lord is close to those of who are a broken heart and saves such as are crushed for sorrow for sin and are humbly and thoroughly penitent. Many evils confront the righteous, but the Lord delivers him out of them all.
- **Hosea 6:3** Yes, let us know Him; let us be zealous to know the Lord. His going forth is prepared and certain as the dawn, and He will come to us as the rain, as the latter rain that waters the earth.
- **Psalm 90:12** So teach us to number our days that we may get us a heart of wisdom.
- **John 14:1** Do not let your hearts be troubled. You believe in and adhere to and trust in and rely also on me.
- **Psalm 40:1-3** I waited patiently and expectantly for the Lord; and He inclined to me and heard my cry. He drew me up out of a horrible pit, out of the miry clay, and set my feet upon a rock steadying my steps and establishing my goings. And He has put a new song my mouth, a song of praise to

our God. Many shall see and fear and put their trust and confident reliance in the Lord.

- **Proverbs 16:1** The Plans of the mind and orderly thinking belong to man, but from the Lord comes the answer of the tongue.
- **Proverbs 15:30** The light in the eyes (of him whose heart is cheerful) rejoices the hearts of others, and good news nourishes the bones.
- **Psalm 121:1-4** I will lift up my eyes to the hills. From whence shall my help come? My help comes from the Lord, Who made heaven and earth. He will not allow your foot to slip or to be moved; He Who keeps you will not slumber. Behold, He who keeps Israel neither will slumber or sleep.
- **Nehemiah 9:6** You are the Lord, You alone; You have made heaven, the heaven of heavens, with all their host, the earth, and all that is on it, the seas, and all that is in them; And You preserve them all, and the hosts of heaven worship you.
- **Proverbs 15:4** A gentle tongue (with its healing power) is a tree of life, but willful contrariness in it breaks down the spirit.
- **Isaiah 30:15** For thus said the Lord God, the Holy One of Israel: In returning (to Me) and resting (in Me) you shall be saved; in quietness and in (trusting) confidence shall be your strength.
- **Romans 8:38-39** For I am persuaded beyond doubt that neither death nor life, nor angels nor principalities nor things impending and threatening nor things to come, nor powers, Nor height nor depth, nor anything else in all creation will

be able to separate us from the love of God which is in Christ Jesus our Lord.

- **Isaiah 40:31** But those who wait for the Lord (who expect, look for, and hope in Him) shall change and renew their strength and power; they shall lift their wings and mount up as eagles; they shall run and not be weary, they shall walk and not faint or become tired.
- **Nahum 1:7** The Lord is good, a Strength and Stronghold in the day of trouble. He knows those who take refuge and trust in him.
- **Jeremiah 32:17** Alas, Lord God! Behold, you have made the heavens and the earth by Your great power and by your outstretched arm! There is nothing too hard or too wonderful for you.
- **Isaiah 43:2** When you pass through the waters, I will be with you, and through the rivers, they will not overwhelm you; When you walk through the fire, you will not be burned or scorched, nor will the flame kindle upon you.
- **Jonah: 2:7** When my soul fainted upon me, I earnestly and seriously remembered the Lord; and my prayer came to You, into your holy temple.
- **Psalm 16:11** You will show me the path of life; in Your presence is fullness of joy, at Your right hand there are pleasures forevermore.
- **Psalm 30:2-5** O Lord my God, I cried to You and You have healed me. O Lord, You have brought my life up from Sheol (the place of the dead); You have kept me alive, that I should not go down to the pit (the grave). Sing to the Lord, O you saints of His, and give thanks at the remembrance of His holy name. For His anger is but for a moment, but His favor

is for a lifetime or in His favor is life. Weeping may endure for a night, but joy comes in the morning.
- **Matthew 6:34** So do not worry or be anxious about tomorrow, for tomorrow will have worries and anxieties of its own. Sufficient for each day is its own trouble.
- **Psalm 94:19** In the multitude of my (anxious) thoughts within me, Your comforts cheer and delight my soul!
- **Psalm 8:3-4** When I view and consider Your heavens, the work of Your fingers, the moon and the stars, which You have ordained and established, What is man that You are mindful of him, and the son of (earthborn)man that you care for him?
- **John 10:10** The thief comes only in order to steal and kill and destroy. I came that they may have and enjoy life, and have it in abundance (to the full, till it overflows).
- **Isaiah 40:28-29** Have you not known? Have you not heard? The everlasting God, the Lord, the Creator of the ends of the earth, does not faint or grow weary. There is no searching of His understanding. He gives power to the faint and weary, and to him who has no might He increases strength (causing it to multiply and making it to abound).
- **Matthew 11:28** Come to Me, all you who labor and are heavy-laden and overburdened, and I will cause you to rest. (I will ease and relieve and refresh your souls).
- **2 Thessalonians 3:16** Now may the Lord of peace Himself grant you His peace at all times and in all ways (under all circumstances and conditions, whatever comes). The Lord (be) with you all.
- **Isaiah 26:3-4** You will guard him and keep him in perfect and constant peace whose mind is stayed on You, because

he commits himself to You, leans on You, and hopes confidently in You. So trust in the Lord (commit yourself to Him, lean on Him, hope confidently in Him) forever; for the Lord God is an everlasting Rock (the Rock of Ages).
- **Philippians 4:6**—Do not fret or have any anxiety about anything, but in every circumstance and in everything, by prayer and petition (definite requests), with thanksgiving, continue to make your wants known to God.
- **Joshua 1:9** Have not I commanded you? Be strong, vigorous, and very courageous. Be not afraid, neither be dismayed, for the Lord your God is with you wherever you go.
- **1 Peter 5:7** Casting the whole of your care (all your anxieties, all your worries, all your concerns, once and for all) on Him, for He cares for you affectionately and cares about you watchfully.
- **John 14:27** Peace I leave with you; My (own) peace I now give and bequeath to you. Not as the world gives do I give to you. Do not let your hearts be troubled, neither let them be afraid. (Stop allowing yourselves to be agitated and disturbed; and do not permit yourselves to be fearful and intimidated and cowardly and unsettled.)
- **Proverbs 15:15** All the days of the desponding and afflicted are made evil (by anxious thoughts and forebodings), but he who has a glad heart has a continual feast (regardless of circumstances).
- **Psalm 37:4** Delight yourself also in the Lord, and he will give you the desires and secret petitions of your heart.
- **Deuteronomy 31:6** Be strong, courageous, and firm; fear not nor be in terror before them, for it is the Lord your God Who goes with you; He will not fail you or forsake you.

- **Lamentations 3:22-23** It is because of the Lord's mercy and loving-kindness that we are not consumed, because His (tender) compassions fail not. They are new every morning; great and abundant is Your stability and faithfulness.
- **1 Peter 3:4** But let it be the inward adorning and beauty of the hidden person of the heart, with the incorruptible and unfading charm of a gentle and peaceful spirit, which is not anxious or wrought up, but is very precious in the sight of God.
- **Jeremiah 32:27** Behold, I am the Lord, the God of all flesh; is there anything too hard for me?
- **Hebrews 12:28** Let us therefore, receiving a kingdom that is firm and stable and cannot be shaken, offer to God pleasing service and acceptable worship, with modesty and pious care and godly fear and awe.
- **Psalm 55:22** Cast your burden on the Lord (releasing the weight of it) and He will sustain you; He will never allow the (consistently) righteous to be moved (made to slip, fall, or fail).
- **James 4:14** Yet you do not know (the least thing) about what may happen tomorrow. What is the nature of your life? You are (really) but a wisp of vapor (a puff of smoke, a mist) that is visible for a little while and then disappears (into thin air).
- **Deuteronomy 31:8** It is the Lord Who goes before you; He will (march) with you; He will not fail you or let you go or forsake you; (let there be no cowardice or flinching, but) fear not, neither become broken (in spirit-depressed, dismayed, and unnerved with alarm).

- **Matthew 11:28** Come to Me, all you who labor and are heavy-laden and overburdened, and I will cause you to rest. (I will ease and relieve and refresh your souls.)
- **Psalm 41:3** The Lord will sustain, refresh, and strengthen him on his bed of languishing; all his bed You (O Lord) will turn, change, and transform in his illness.
- **Micah 7:7-8** But as for me, I will look to the Lord and confident in Him I will keep watch; I will wait with hope and expectancy for the God of my salvation; my God will hear me. Rejoice not against me, O my enemy! When I fall, I shall arise; when I sit in darkness, the Lord shall be a light to me.
- **Matthew 28:20** Teaching them to observe everything that I have commanded you, and behold, I am with you all the days (perpetually, uniformly, and on every occasion), to the (very) close and consummation of the age.
- **John 16:33** I have told you these things, so that in me you may have (perfect) peace and confidence. In the world you have tribulation and trials and distress and frustration; but be of good cheer (take courage; be confident, certain, undaunted)! For I have overcome the world. (I have deprived it of power to harm you and have conquered it for you.)
- **Psalm 62:6** He only is my Rock and my Salvation; He is my Defense and my Fortress, I shall not be moved.
- **Philippians 4:13** I have strength for all things in Christ Who empowers me (I am ready for anything and equal to anything through Him Who infuses inner strength into me; I am self-sufficient in Christ's sufficiency).

- **Proverbs 8:17** I love those who love me, and those who seek me early and diligently shall find me.
- **Matthew 19:26** But Jesus looked at them and said, With men this is impossible, but all things are possible with God.
- **Exodus 15:26** If you will diligently hearken to the voice of the Lord your God and will do what is right in his sight, and will listen to and obey his commandments and keep all his statutes, I will put none of the diseases upon you which I brought upon the Egyptians, for I am the Lord Who heals you.
- **Psalm 42:8** Yet the Lord will command His loving-kindness in the daytime, and in the night His song shall be with me, a prayer to the God of my life.
- **Psalm 34:6-7** This poor man cried, and the Lord heard him, and saved him out of all his troubles. The Angel of the Lord encamps around those who fear him (who revere and worship Him with awe) and each of them he delivers.
- **Psalm 125:1** Those Who trust in, lean on, and confidently hope in the Lord are like Mount Zion, which cannot be moved but abides and stands fast forever.
- **Psalm 118:1** O Give thanks to the Lord, for He is good; for His mercy and loving-kindness endure forever!
- **Malachi 4:2** But unto you who revere and worshipfully fear My name shall the Sun of Righteousness arise with healing in His wings and His beams, and you shall go forth and gambol like calves (released) from the stall and leap for joy.
- **Proverbs 18:10** The name of the Lord is a strong tower; the (consistently) righteous man (upright and in right standing

with God) runs into it and is safe, high (above evil) and strong.

- **Psalm 138:7** Though I walk in the midst of trouble, You will revive me; You will stretch forth your hand against the wrath of my enemies, and Your right hand will save me.
- **Psalm 5:12** For You, Lord, will bless the (uncompromisingly) righteous (him who is upright and in right standing with You); as with a shield You will surround him with goodwill (pleasure and favor).
- **Psalm 4:8** In peace I will both lie down and sleep, for You, Lord, alone make me dwell in safety and confident trust.
- **Deuteronomy 33:12** The beloved of the Lord shall dwell in safety by Him; He covers him all the day long, and makes His dwelling between his shoulders.
- **2 Samuel 22:29** For You, O Lord, are my Lamp; the Lord lightens my darkness.
- **Habakkuk 3:17-19** Though the fig tree does not blossom and there is no fruit on the vines, (though) the product of the olive fails and the fields yield no food, though the flock is cut off from the fold and there are no cattle in the stalls, Yet I will rejoice in the Lord; I will exult in the (victorious) God of my salvation! The Lord God is my strength, my personal bravery, and my invincible army; He makes my feet like hinds feet and will make me to walk (not to stand still in terror, but to walk) and make (spiritual) progress upon my high places (of trouble, suffering, or responsibility)!
- **Romans 5:3** Moreover (let us also be full of joy now!) let us exult and triumph in our troubles and rejoice in our sufferings, knowing that pressure and affliction and hardship produce patient and unswerving endurance.

- **Mark 5:34** And He said to her, Daughter, your faith (your trust and confidence in Me, springing from faith in God) has restored you to health. Go in peace and be continually healed and freed from your (distressing bodily) disease.
- **Psalm 27:1** The Lord is my Light and my Salvation-whom shall I fear or dread? The Lord is the Refuge and Stronghold of my life-of whom shall I be afraid?
- **Psalm 42:11** Why are you cast down, O my inner self? And why should you moan over me and be disquieted within me? Hope in God and wait expectantly for Him, for I shall yet praise Him, Who is the help of my countenance, and my God.
- **Isaiah 41:13** For I the Lord your God hold your right hand; I am the Lord, Who says to you, Fear not; I will help you!
- **2 Corinthians 4:8** We are hedged in (pressed) on every side (troubled and oppressed in every way), but not cramped or crushed; we suffer embarrassments and are perplexed and unable to find a way out, but not driven to despair.
- **Ephesians 3:16-20** May He grant you out of the rich treasury of his glory to be strengthened and reinforced with mighty power in the inner man by the (Holy) Spirit (Himself indwelling your innermost being and personality). May Christ through your faith (actually) dwell (settle down, abide, make his permanent home) in your hearts! May you be rooted deep in love and founded securely on love, that you may have the power and be strong to apprehend and grasp with all the saints (God's devoted people, the experience of that love) what is the breadth and length and height and depth (of it); (That you may really come) to know (practically, through experience for yourselves)

the love of Christ, which far surpasses mere knowledge (without experience); that you may be filled (through all your being) unto all the fullness of God (may have the richest measure of the divine Presence, and become a body wholly filled and flooded with God Himself)! Now to Him Who, by (in consequence of) the (action of his) power that is at work within us, is able to (carry out his purpose and) do superabundantly, far over and above all that we (dare) ask or think (infinitely beyond our highest prayers, desires, thoughts, hopes or dreams).

- **2 Peter 1:2-3** May grace (God's favor) and peace (which is perfect well-being all necessary good, all spiritual prosperity, and freedom from fears and agitating passions and moral conflicts) be multiplied to you in (the full, personal, precise, and correct) knowledge of God and Jesus our Lord. For His divine power has bestowed upon us all things that (are requisite and suited) to life and godliness, through the (full, personal) knowledge of him Who called us by and to His own glory and excellence (virtue).
- **Isaiah 41:10** Fear not (there is nothing to fear), for I am with you; do not look around you in terror and be dismayed, for I am your God, I will strengthen and harden you to difficulties, yes, I will help you; yes, I will hold you up and retain you with My (victorious) right hand of rightness and justice.
- **Daniel 10:19** And he said, O man greatly beloved, fear not! Peace be to you! Be strong, yes, be strong. And when he had spoken to me, I was strengthened and said, Let my lord speak for you have strengthened me.
- **Psalm 103:2-3** Bless (affectionately, gratefully praise) the Lord, O my soul, and forget not (one of) all His benefits.

Who forgives (every one of) all your iniquities, Who heals (each one of) all your diseases.

- **Isaiah 46:4** Even to your old age I am He, and even to hair white with age will I carry you. I have made, and I will bear; yes, I will carry and will save you.
- **Psalm 73:23-26** Nevertheless I am continually with You; You do hold my right hand. You will guide me with Your counsel, and afterward receive me to honor and glory. Whom have I in heaven but You? And I have no delight or desire on earth besides You. My flesh and my heart may fail, but God is the Rock and firm Strength of my heart and my Portion forever.
- **Psalm 27:13-14** What would have become of me had I not believed that I would see the Lord's goodness in the land of the living! Wait and hope for and expect the Lord; be brave and of good courage and let your heart be stout and enduring. Yes, wait for and hope for and expect the Lord.
- **Psalm 113:3** From the rising of the sun to the going down of it and from east to west, the name of the Lord is to be praised!
- **Philippians 4:4** Rejoice in the Lord always, (delight, gladden yourselves in Him); again, I say, Rejoice!
- **Psalm 118:24** This is the day which the Lord has brought about; we will rejoice and be glad in it.
- **Psalm 116:1-9** I love the Lord, because He has heard (and now hears) my voice and my supplications. Because He has inclined His ear to me, therefore will I call upon Him as long as I live. The cords and sorrows of death were around me, and the terrors of Sheol (the place of the dead) had been laid hold of me; I suffered anguish and grief (trouble and

sorrow). Then called I upon the name of the Lord; O Lord, I beseech You, save my life and deliver me! Gracious is the Lord, and righteous; yes, our God is merciful. The Lord preserves the simple; I was brought low, and He helped and saved me. Return to your rest, O my soul, for the Lord has dealt bountifully with you. For You have delivered my life from death, my eyes from tears, and my feet from stumbling and falling. I will walk before the Lord in the land of the living.

- **Psalm 23** The Lord is my Shepherd (to feed, guide, and shield me), I shall not lack. He makes me lie down in (fresh, tender) green pastures; He leads me besides the still and restful waters. He refreshes and restores my life (my self); He leads me in the paths of righteousness (uprightness and right standing with Him-not for my earning it, but) for His names sake. Yes, though I walk through the (deep, sunless) valley of the shadow of death, I will fear or dread no evil, for You are with me; Your rod (to protect) and Your staff (to guide), they comfort me. You prepare a table before me in the presence of my enemies. You anoint my head with oil; my (brimming) cup runs over. Surely only goodness, mercy, and unfailing love shall follow me all the days of my life, and through the length of my days the house of the Lord (and His presence) shall be my dwelling place.

- **Psalm 91** He who dwells in the secret place of the Most High shall remain stable and fixed under the shadow of the Almighty (Whose power no foe can withstand). I will say of the Lord, He is my Refuge and my Fortress, my God; on Him I lean and rely, and in Him I (confidently) trust! For (then) He will deliver you from the snare of the fowler and from the deadly pestilence. (Then) He will cover you with His pinions, and under His wings shall you trust and find refuge; His truth and His faithfulness are a shield and a buckler. You shall not be afraid of the terror of the night, nor of the arrow (the evil plots and slanders of the wicked) that flies by day. Nor of the pestilence that stalks in darkness, nor of the destruction and sudden death that surprise and lay waste at noonday. A thousand may fall at your side, and ten thousand at your right hand, but it shall not come near you. Only a spectator shall you be (yourself inaccessible in the secret place of the Most High) as you witness the reward of the wicked. Because you have made the Lord your refuge, and the Most High your dwelling place, There shall no evil befall you, nor any plague or calamity come near your tent. For He will give His angels (special) charge over you to accompany and defend and preserve you in all your ways (of obedience and service).They shall bear you up on their hands, lest you dash your foot against a stone. You shall tread upon the lion and adder; the young lion and the serpent shall you trample underfoot. Because He has set His love upon Me, therefore will I deliver him; I will set him on high, because he knows and understands My name (has a personal knowledge of My mercy, love, and kindness-trusts and relies on Me, knowing I will never forsake him, no, never). He shall call upon Me, and I will answer him; I will be with him in trouble, I will deliver him and honor him. With long life will I satisfy him and show him My salvation.

- **Psalm 139** O Lord, you have searched me (thoroughly) and have known me. You know my downsitting and my uprising.

You understand my thought afar off. You sift and search out my path and my lying down, and You are acquainted with all my ways. For there is not a work in my tongue (still unuttered), but, behold, O Lord, You know it altogether. You have beset me and shut me in-behind and before, and You have laid your hand upon me. Your (infinite) knowledge is too wonderful for me; it is high above me, I cannot reach it. Where could I go from your spirit? Or where could I flee from Your presence? If I ascend up into heaven, You are there; if I make my bed in Sheol (the place of the dead), behold, You are there. If I take the wings of the morning or dwell in the uttermost parts of the sea, Even there shall your hand lead me, and Your right hand shall hold me. If I say, Surely the darkness shall cover me and the night shall be (the only) light about me, Even the darkness hides nothing from You, but the night shines as the day; the darkness and the light are both alike to You. For You did form my inward parts; You did knit me together in my mother's womb. I will confess and praise You for You are fearful and wonderful and for the awful wonder of my birth! Wonderful are Your works, and that my inner self knows right well. My frame was not hidden from You when I was being formed in secret (and) intricately and curiously wrought (as if embroidered with various colors) in the depths of the earth (a region of darkness and mystery). Your eyes saw my unformed substance, and in Your book all the days (of my life) were written before ever they took shape, when as yet there were none of them. How precious and weighty also are Your thoughts to me, O God! How vast is the sum of them! If I could count them, they would be more in number than the sand. When I awoke, (could I count to the end) I would still be with You. If You would (only) slay the wicked, O God, and the men of blood depart from me. Who speak against You wickedly, Your enemies who take Your name in vain! Do I not hate them, O Lord, who hate You? And am I not grieved and do I not loathe those who rise up against You? I hate them with perfect hatred; they have become my enemies. Search me (thoroughly), O God, and know my heart! Try me and know my thoughts! And see if there is any wicked or hurtful way in me, and lead me in the way everlasting.

- **Ecclesiastes 3:1-2** To Everything there is a season, and a time for every matter or purpose under heaven: A time to be born and a time to die, a time to plant and a time to pluck up what is planted.

- **Psalm 30:11-12** You have turned my mourning into dancing for me; You have put off my sackcloth and girded me with gladness. To the end that my tongue and my heart and everything glorious within me may sing praise to You and not be silent. O Lord my God, I will give thanks to you forever.

- **Psalm 20:4-5** May he grant you according to your heart's desire and fulfill all your plans. We will (shout in) triumph at your salvation and victory, and in the name of our God we will set up our banners. May the Lord fulfill all your petitions.

- **Psalm 33:1-3** Rejoice in the Lord, O you righteous; for praise is becoming and appropriate for those who are upright (in heart). Give thanks to the Lord with the lyre; sing praises to Him with the harp of ten strings. Sing to him a new song; play skillfully with a loud and joyful song.

- **Psalm 32:7-11** You are a hiding place for me; You, Lord, preserve me from trouble, You surround me with songs and shouts of deliverance. I (the Lord) will instruct you and teach you in the way you should go; I will counsel you with my eye upon you. Be not like the horse or the mule, which lack understanding, which must have their mouths held firm with bit and bridle, or else they will not come with you. Many are the sorrows of the wicked, but he who trusts in, relies on, and confidently leans on the Lord shall be compassed about with mercy and with loving-kindness. Be glad in the Lord and rejoice you righteous (you who are upright and right standing with Him); shout for joy, all you upright in heart!
- **Psalm 63:1, 3-4** O God, You are my God, earnestly will I seek You; my inner self thirsts for You, my flesh longs and is faint for You, in a dry and weary land where no water is. Because Your loving-kindness is better than life, my lips shall praise You. So will I bless You while I live; I will lift up my hands in Your name.
- **Psalm 63:6-8** When I remember You upon my bed and meditate on You in the night watches. For You have been my help, and in the shadow of Your wings will I rejoice. My whole being follows hard after You and clings closely to You; Your right hand upholds me.
- **Psalm 68:19-20** Blessed be the Lord, Who bears our burdens and carries us day by day, even the God Who is our salvation! God is to us a God of deliverances and salvation; and to God the Lord belongs escape from death (setting us free).
- **Psalm 104:33-34** I will sing to the Lord as long as I live; I will sing praise to my God while I have any being. May my

meditation be sweet to Him; as for me, I will rejoice in the Lord.

- **Psalm 73:23-24, 26** Nevertheless I am continually with you; You do hold my right hand. You will guide me with Your counsel, and afterward receive me in honor and glory. My flesh and my heart may fail, but God is the Rock and firm Strength of my heart and my Portion forever.
- **Psalm 118:15-17** The voice of rejoicing and salvation is in the tents and private dwellings of the righteous; the right hand of the Lord does valiantly and achieves strength! The right hand of the Lord is exalted; The right hand of the Lord does valiantly and achieves strength! I shall not die but live, and shall declare the works and recount the illustrious acts of the Lord.
- **Psalm 119:67, 71** Before I was afflicted I went astray, but now Your word do I keep (hearing, receiving, loving, and obeying it). It is good for me that I have been afflicted, that I might learn Your statutes.
- **Song of Solomon 2:11-12** For, behold, the winter is past; the rain is over and gone. The flowers appear on the earth; the time of the singing (of birds) has come, and the voice of the turtledove is heard in our land.
- **Psalm 8:1-2** O Lord, our Lord, how excellent (majestic and glorious) is Your name in all the earth! You have set your glory on (or above) the heavens. Out of the mouths of babes and unweaned infants You have established strength because of Your foes, that you might silence the enemy and the avenger.
- **Psalm 103:1-4** Bless (Affectionately, gratefully praise) the Lord, O my soul; and all that is (deepest) within me, bless His holy name! Bless the Lord, O my soul, and forget not

(one of) all his benefits-Who forgives every one of) all your iniquities, Who heals (each one of) all your diseases. Who redeems your life from the pit and corruption, Who beautifies, dignifies, and crowns you with loving-kindness and tender mercy.

- **Exodus 15:2** The Lord is my Strength and my Song, and He has become my Salvation; This is my God, and I will praise Him, my father's God and I will exalt Him.

(Psalm 126 is the scripture passage that *Rejoicing through the Tears* was named after.

- **Psalm 126** When the Lord brought back the captives to Zion, we were like those who dream (it seemed so unreal). Then were our mouths filled with laughter, and our tongues with singing. Then they said among the nations, The Lord has done great things for them. The Lord has done great things for us! We are glad! Turn to freedom our captivity and restore our fortunes, O Lord, as the streams in the South (the Negeb) are restored by torrents. They who sow in tears shall reap in joy and singing. He who goes fort bearing seed and weeping (at needing his precious supply of grain for sowing) shall doubtless come again with rejoicing, bringing his sheaves with him.
- **Psalm 66:8-9** Bless our God, O peoples, give Him grateful thanks and make the voice of His praise be heard. Who put and keep us among the living, and has not allowed our feet to slip.
- **Job 8:21** He will yet fill your mouth with laughter and your lips with joyful shouting.

- **Psalm 9:1-2** I will praise you, O Lord, with my whole heart; I will show forth (recount and tell aloud) all Your marvelous works and wonderful deeds! I will rejoice in You and be in high spirits; I will sing praise to Your name, O Most High!
- **Isaiah 61:1-3** The Spirit of the Lord God is upon me, because the Lord has anointed and qualified me to preach the Gospel of good tidings to the meek, the poor, and afflicted; He has sent me to bind up and heal the brokenhearted, to proclaim liberty to the (physical and spiritual) captives and the opening of the prison and of the eyes to those who are bound, To proclaim the acceptable year of the Lord (the year of His favor) and the day of vengeance of our God, to comfort all who mourn, To grant (consolation and joy) to those who mourn in Zion-to give them an ornament of beauty instead of ashes, the oil of joy instead of mourning, the garment of praise instead of a heavy, burdened, and failing spirit-that they may be called oaks of righteousness (lofty, strong, and magnificent, distinguished for uprightness, justice, and right standing with God), the planting of the Lord, that He may be glorified
- **Psalm 63:3-5** Because Your loving-kindness is better than life, my lips shall praise You. So will I bless you while I live; I will lift up my hands in Your name. My whole being shall be satisfied as with marrow and fatness; and my mouth shall praise You with joyful lips.
- **Psalm 81:1-2** Sing aloud to God our Strength! Shout for joy to the God of Jacob! Raise a song, sound the timbrel, the sweet lyre with the harp.

- **Psalms 89:15-16** Blessed (happy, fortunate, to be envied) are the people who know the joyful sound (who understand and appreciate the spiritual blessings symbolized by the feasts); they walk, O Lord, in the light and favor of Your countenance! In Your name they rejoice all the day, and in Your righteousness they are exalted.
- **Psalm 92:1-4** It is a good and delightful thing to give thanks to the Lord, to sing praises (with musical accompaniment) to Your name, O Most High, To show forth your loving kindness in the morning and Your faithfulness by night. With an instrument of ten strings and with the lute, with a solemn sound upon the lyre. For You, O Lord, have made me glad by Your works; at the deeds of Your hands I joyfully sing.
- **Psalm 100** Make a joyful noise to the Lord, all you lands! Serve the Lord with gladness! Come before His presence with singing! Know that the Lord is God! It is He Who has made us; not we ourselves. We are His people and the sheep of His pasture. Enter into His gates with thanksgiving and a thank offering and into His courts with praise! Be thankful and say so to Him, bless and affectionately praise His name! For the Lord is good; His mercy and loving-kindness are everlasting, His faithfulness and truth endure to all generations.
- **Psalm 150** Praise the Lord! Praise God in His sanctuary; praise Him in the heavens of His power! Praise Him for His mighty acts; praise Him according to the abundance of His greatness! Praise Him with trumpet sound; praise Him with lute and harp! Praise Him with tambourine and

dance; praise Him with stringed and wind instruments or flutes! Praise Him with resounding cymbals; praise Him with loud clashing cymbals! Let everything that has breath and every breath of life praise the Lord! Praise the Lord! (Hallelujah!)

In Conclusion

After reading these Scriptures, what more is there to say? God's word is truth and will set you free from any heartache. I can't help but think of Psalm 42:11: "Why are you downcast, O my soul? Why so disturbed within me? Put your hope in God, for I will yet praise him, my Savior and my God." That Scripture says it all. Nothing can ever separate you from God's love. These aren't just empty words. They carry with them the ability to overcome any sorrow.

I pray that the next time you see a rainbow you will remember that it was God's promise in the beginning, and he has a promise for your life, also. He is full of compassion and mercy, and his faithfulness is new every morning. There is no problem too big for our God. If a tiny sparrow cannot fall to the ground without him knowing it, there is never one single tear that you shed that he doesn't know about.

No matter what you are going through in your life, God is there to comfort you. Abide in him. Run to him, because he is a strong tower. There is safety in him. He will comfort you in your wilderness journey, and he will bring you *through* into a land flowing with milk and honey, regardless of your situation. He can fill you with his presence that surpasses all human understanding. Learn to draw upon his strength. Keep worshipping him, even when there seems to be nothing to be thankful for. He will break through your darkness and abundant joy will appear. He doesn't just *give* life. He *is* life!

I pray that God will anoint this book and use it to heal the brokenhearted, bind up your wounds, and set your spirit free to worship him through any adversity. You will be able to say with me that, though I fall, I will rise, and while I am down, my heart and hands will be lifted up. Learn to embrace your storm, knowing that God is in full control. Perfect love casts out all fear. He will keep you in perfect peace if you keep your thoughts on him. **1 John 4:18**

There is one final thought that is of great importance and is a key element in making your faith work for you. Without it, this book loses much of its purpose. God's word clearly points out, that the only way you can be assured of your eternity in heaven is through his son, Jesus Christ. God gave his only son to die for your sins. There's nothing complicated about it. In fact, it's as natural and easy as taking your next breath. You see, God did all this for you so that you don't have to do anything but recognize that you are a sinner, acknowledge that Jesus died for your sins, and accept his free gift of eternal life; you can't get to heaven by being good, because it's not about you.

There's nothing you can do to earn salvation. It's simply a free gift of God's grace. The Bible says all have sinned and come short of the glory of God. Just like there's no way of getting around cancer, there's no other way to heaven. Jesus is the only way. No one is worthy within themselves. Money and fame will not satisfy. Only Jesus will satisfy that longing in your heart. Jesus loves you so much that he was willing to die for you. His love is awesome. He loves you so! The Bible says that God has given us the freedom to choose for ourselves, but we will have to pay the consequences for the choice that we make. God said he has set before us blessings and cursings, life and death. Choose life! Proverbs 30:19

Although this book is written with full anticipation of my recovering from cancer, I must face the truth that there will be those who will not. The Bible says that it is appointed for man once to die and then the judgment. This section of *Rejoicing through the Tears* is written to give you the assurance of all that heaven has to offer. If you find yourself relating more to this part of this book, just remember that heaven is a very real place. It is your final hope for all of eternity if you know Jesus. It is a land of no more tears, pain, or longing for those we love and miss for the Bible says that the old order of things has passed away. Jesus said, "In my Father's house are many mansions." The Bible says that now we see dimly, like through a glass, but soon we will see him face to face, and we will know him, even as he already knows us. He is fully aware of every sigh you take, and he cares for you so much more than you know. In heaven, there will be no more sun, because Jesus will be the everlasting light. He is the great I Am, the Alpha and the Omega, and the Beginning and the End. He is the Lamb that was slain. He is the Bright and Morning Star. He will be high and lifted up! What a glorious hope!

I get the feeling that he knows full well what he is doing, and he has everything under control! Scripture says that the pathway of the just grows brighter and brighter, and we will go from glory to glory. God will never leave us or forsake us. He never leaves us without hope. He is preparing a place for us more glorious than we could ever imagine, hope, or think. Our humanly minds cannot take it all in or contain it! It will be the biggest homecoming, and we will be reunited with our loved ones. We can then say, "It is well with my soul." We will be home at last! What a celebration that will be—one celebration I don't want to miss!

Once we enter those pearly gates, we will walk those golden streets that look like transparent glass not only with our loved ones, but with Jesus himself. We will then know perfect love. We will cast our crowns at his feet and walk with him by the River of Life around the glassy sea. We will join with the angels and all the saints from down through countless ages singing, "Holy, Holy, Holy" and "Worthy is the lamb, who was slain." Eye hath not seen nor ear heard the glory that awaits us on the other side. It will be a place of great rejoicing and worship!

As I reflect upon the bright light that I experienced in the body scan, I realize it was everything about who he is, and he was just showing me who I am and my incredible worth. He was just being the God of light, which is exactly who he is. It was his way of wrapping me in his love and saying to me, "Thou art highly esteemed, My Child. I am here for you. I love you with an everlasting love. I am the glory and lifter of your head. You are a precious jewel in my crown." He paid a great price for me, and he paid a great price for you. He is no respecter of persons. You have incredible worth in his eyes.

I don't know if I'll die today or if I will live to be one hundred. I've taken care of the most important issues dealing with eternity, and now I can live my life to the fullest each day while on earth. The Bible says in Hebrews 12:1, to run the race here on earth and we have a great cloud of witnesses in heaven that are cheering us on. I know that everything I do for him is worthwhile, and I can never get out of his presence. He is the glory and lifter of my head. He came to give me life to the full, pressed down and shaken together and running over! I was glad when they said, Psalm 122:1 "Let us go to the house of the Lord, for in his presence is fullness of joy!" I can live with confidence in this new life that God has given me, because I know that the bright light that I experienced in the body scan was only a foretaste of what I have to look forward to. I now know that all of this singing, dancing, and rejoicing I'm doing here on earth is simply an audition until my voice is joined with that heavenly choir that you and I will be a part of!

Scripture:

I was glad when they said to me; Let us go to the house of the Lord!

Psalm 122:1

And just as it is appointed for (all) men once to die, and after that the (certain) judgment.

Hebrews 9:27

Therefore then, since we are surrounded by so great a cloud of witnesses, let us strip off and throw aside every encumbrance (unnecessary weight) and that sin which so readily clings to and entangles us, and let us run with patient endurance and steady and active persistence the appointed course of the race that is set before us.

Hebrews 12:1

Let your character or moral disposition be free from love of money (including greed, avarice, lust, and craving for earthly possessions) and be satisfied with your present (circumstances and with what you have); for He (God) Himself has said, I will not

in any way fail you or give you up nor leave you without support. (I will) not, I will not, I will not in any degree leave you helpless nor forsake nor let you down (relax my hold on you)! (Assuredly not!)

Hebrews 13:5

I saw the Lord sitting upon a throne, high and lifted up, and the skirts of His train filled the temple.

Isaiah 6:1

Your sun shall no more go down, nor shall your moon withdraw itself, for the Lord shall be your everlasting light, and the days of your mourning shall be ended.

Isaiah 60:20

Where could I go from Your Spirit? Or where could I flee from your presence?

Psalm 139:7

Namely, the righteousness of God which comes by believing with personal trust and confident reliance on Jesus Christ for all who believe. For there is no distinction. Since all have sinned and are falling short of the honor and glory which God bestows and receives.

Romans 3:22-23

I call heaven and earth to witness this day against you that I have set before you life and death, the blessings and the curses; therefore choose life that you and your descendants may live.

Deuteronomy 30:19

Now to Him Who by the power that is at work within us, is able to do superabundantly, far over and above all that we (dare) ask or think (infinitely beyond our highest prayers, desires, thoughts, hopes, or dreams)

Ephesians 3:20

But, on the contrary, as the Scripture says, what eye has not seen and ear has not heard and has not entered into the heart of man, (all that) God has prepared for those who love Him

1 Corinthians 2:9

In My Father's house there are many dwelling places (homes). If it were not so, I would have told you; for I am going away to prepare a place for you.

John 14:2

For now we are looking in a mirror that gives only a dim (blurred) reflection, but then, we shall see in reality and face to face! Now I know in part (imperfectly), but then I shall know and understand fully and clearly, even in the same manner as I have been fully and clearly known and understood by God. And so faith, hope, love abide these three; but the greatest of these is love.

Corinthians 13:12-13

Give, and (gifts) will be given to you; good measure, pressed down, shaken together, and running over, will they pour into your bosom. For with the measure you deal out, it will be measured back to you.

Luke 6:38

But you, O Lord, are a shield for me, my glory, and the lifter of my head.

Psalm 3:3

At once I came under the (Holy) Spirit's power, and behold, a throne stood in heaven, with One seated on the throne! And He Who sat there appeared like (the crystalline brightness of jasper and the fiery sardius, and, encircling the throne there was a halo that looked like a rainbow of emerald.

Revelation 4:2-3

The twenty four elders fall prostrate before Him Who is sitting on the throne, and they worship Him Who lives forever and ever; and they throw down their crowns before the throne, crying out, Worthy are You, our Lord and God, to receive the glory and the honor and dominion, for You created all things; by Your will they were brought into being and were created.

Revelation 4:10-11

I, Jesus, have sent My messenger (angel) to you to witness and to give you assurance of these things for the churches. I am the Root (the Source) and the Offspring of David, the radiant and brilliant Morning star.

Revelation 22:16

The wilderness and the dry land shall be glad; the desert shall rejoice and blossom like the rose and the autumn crocus. It shall blossom abundantly and rejoice even with joy and singing. The glory of Lebanon shall be given to it, the excellency of Mount Carmel and the Plain of Sharon. They shall see the glory of the Lord, the majesty and splendor and excellency of our God. Strengthen the weak hands and make firm the feeble and tottering knees. Say to those who are of a fearful and hasty heart, Be strong, fear not! Behold, your God will come with vengeance; with the recompense of God He will come and save you. Then the eyes of the blind shall be opened, and the ears of the deaf shall be unstopped. Then shall the lame man leap like a hart, and the tongue of the dumb shall sing for joy. For waters shall break forth in the wilderness and streams in the desert. And the burning sand and the mirage shall become a pool, and the thirsty ground springs of water; in the haunt of jackals, where they lay resting, shall be grass with reeds and rushes. And a highway shall be there, and a way; and it shall be called the Holy Way. The unclean shall not pass over it, but it shall be for the redeemed; the wayfaring men, yes, the simple ones and fools, shall not err in it and lose their way. No lion shall be there, nor shall any ravenous beast come up on it; they shall not be found there. But the redeemed shall walk on it. And the ransomed of the Lord shall return and come to Zion with singing, and everlasting joy shall be upon their heads; they shall obtain joy and gladness, and sorrow and sighing shall flee away.

Isaiah 35

Brenda George

My Prayer

My precious Jesus,

You are holy. There is no one like you. I love you with my whole heart. You are so worthy of my praise. Great is your faithfulness, O God! I thank you so much for your glorious presence in my life even when I don't deserve it. Because of your grace and love for me, you have changed my life completely. You have turned my sorrow into joy. I will worship you until the end of my days.

 You have given me this book, and now I'm giving it back to you for your glory alone, O Lord! I pray that everyone who reads it will come away with a sense of your presence in their lives and will be touched by your great love for them. As you walk into their lives, I pray that you will comfort them with the comfort that only you can give and that their bitter tears will be transformed with hope, peace, and shouts of joy!

Amen.

The Blessing

May the Lord bless you and keep you;
May he make his face to shine upon you and be gracious to you;
May he lift up his countenance on you and give you peace.

Numbers 6:22-27

CPSIA information can be obtained at www.ICGtesting.com
Printed in the USA
BVOW08s1034190516

448655BV00001B/8/P